Greening of the Soul

A DREAMSTAIRWAY BOOK

Greening of the Soul

by

Raymond Foster

DREAMSTAIRWAY

ISBN 978-1-907091-07-0

British Library Cataloguing in Publication Data
A catalogue record for this book is available from the British Library

First published in the UK by Dreamstairway
© Raymond Foster 2009

www.dreamstairway.co.uk

Contents

Raymond Foster is a former forester and a poet

INTRODUCTION

A Personal Search for Susila Budhi Dharma

This account is about the rediscovery of the human soul – of my soul. My search began by way of an interest in ecology and the fate of the earth, but it does not include any recipes for industry or agriculture or forestry, because such things are really matters for science, and they are already known or readily knowable. I have concluded that in order to gain an understanding of the earth's real needs it is necessary to gain an equal and parallel understanding of one's own true self. Greening of the soul, on a worldwide scale, would equate to greening of the world.

Ever since the mythical days of Eden the progress of the world and the way we look after it seems to have been downhill, a slow deterioration that has kept pace with the development of human brainpower. This paradox is everywhere apparent: as brainpower increases, stewardship of the planet suffers. Science, it seems, does not really have the answer after all; perhaps the world is already suffering from a surfeit of clever brains, scientific theories and directives. Nature, after all, can burgeon on its own, without a single human brain cell to order it.

If a fresh approach is needed, it might be helpful to explore exactly what is meant by the state of Eden, what it meant in the infancy of humankind, and what it would mean today if it could be regained. It seems plain to me that, if people were indeed intended to "have dominion" over all the other life-forms, they, or we, no longer exercise that right as we should. Even well-meaning individuals, it seems, can no longer live in cooperation with nature, but seem instead to be forever working against it. The world has always functioned on a downwards-dependence of instinct, with a spiritual hierarchy cne layer upon another, all finally resting on the strength of materiality. The burden, it seems, has become too heavy for the regenerative instincts of the earth to cope with, and its natural resources are no longer able satisfactorily to sustain the full complement of life-forms. As far as humankind is concerned, another direction of dependence must be sought: another source of inspiration apart from materiality.

It has been said that you cannot change the world without first changing yourself. Wholeness is the key; but wholeness is a very difficult principle to pin down. No sooner does one begin to study any subject with "wholeness" in mind, starting with this bit and that bit, "wholeness" recedes bit by bit, until it ceases to exist. It does not seem possible to be scientific about "wholeness". Speaking as a former forester, I would say that a sustainable forest needs to be considered as a whole; but to be really meaningful that "whole" must include the people who propose to manage it. The centre of gravity or the basic life-principle of an influential person tends to become the centre of gravity of whatever is being influenced. When the innermost being of a forest manager is fragmented, his forest too will be fragmented. In order to have an influence towards wholeness, it will be necessary to acquire wholeness for oneself, on the inner plane.

In the quest for wholeness, a dilemma very quickly arises, an all-important point that is completely overlooked by most people today: if you have an *intention* to achieve wholeness, that intention itself creates the need for a kind of analysis that destroys the possibility of wholeness; to *analyse* something is to break it down into understandable parts; in this way your own will becomes a hindrance rather than a help. Perhaps it could be summed up by borrowing a myth from the religious tradition of Java: Adam was said to have had two sons, *Sahid Anwar,* the obedient or submissive son, and *Sahid Anwas,* the disobedient or wilful son. To attempt to alter one's own inner state, or anything else on a holistic scale, using the power of *will,* aligns one with *Anwas.* The point I am making is that only the obedient or submissive son *Anwar* can re-approach Eden and bring about the necessary change. One must be spiritually submissive in order to become dominant in a practical way that should be beneficial to that part of creation that is under our stewardship.

INTRODUCTION

Deserts on earth are said to reflect the spiritual condition of humankind. Large areas of what we might call the human soul have become barren and fruitless as material acquisitions increase, taking out of the world more than it can replace. Eventually the resources of the world will falter and fail, and this downwards spiral of failure needs to be checked before it becomes too widespread to mend. The point I am making is that ordinary people may acquire an inner state of wholeness that can have an influence on the world's resources, when everything of nature can fall readily into place. This truly human state will mark the commencement of *Susila Budhi Dharma* – the most appropriate way of living on earth, a way which involves submission towards an inner source of spiritual guidance.

"I have found the narrow path known of old, that stretches far away. By this path the sages who know the Spirit ascend to the regions of heaven and thence to liberation. The path is adorned with white and blue, yellow and green and red. This is the path of the seers of Brahman".

Yajnavalkya

1 : ZEN AND THE GREEN MAN

Ancient Instinct and the World's Needs

> Amidst those dreary miles of thorny thickets
> jacketing parched plains and searing river valleys
> of Capricorn in Africa,
> sequestered haunts of antelope and leopard
> where paths are few and people seldom venture,
> a welcoming sight among repelling thorns:
> the *mupangara* bush with tassels pink and yellow
> to decorate the hats of chiefs.

As a young forester new to the African bush poetic sentiments sometimes vied to override more practical needs. Landmarks, even distinctive trees and bushes such as the pretty *mupangara* (*Dichrostachys glomerata)* were few, and this could be a problem. I soon discovered that the best way not to become lost or start walking in circles, was to adopt an attitude of patient confidence – a kind of submission to an unseen guiding hand. This attitude, I found, would always steer me where I wanted to go, without having constantly to be thinking about direction. Later on, I found that it worked equally well in dense rainforest; and later on still, that it worked in urban surroundings too, even in strange cities.

That I had "discovered" some sort of instinct, I had no doubt. But was it a truly human instinct, or an animal instinct, or even a plant instinct? I had no doubt too that this guidance – so faint and rusty with disuse – was the same guidance that allowed man at the dawn of time – or even hunter-gatherers of the present day – to roam the earth in search of food, and then to find the way back home. Only very slowly did it dawn on me that this gentle nudging could possibly be a stirring of the soul, for so long suppressed. And if this soul could really come to awareness, and if the soul *knew* what needed to be known, then not only personal problems but the major problems facing the world – problems of natural resources, of good stewardship, of good relations – could soon belong to the past.

Several years later an English farmer asked Pak Subuh Sumohadiwidjojo, the founder of *Subud*, whether he considered that a general return to organic farming methods was necessary. His reply was: "Simply follow the *latihan kejiwaan* (the actions of your awakened soul), and after a while, if you are a farmer, you will automatically know what to do, and what the earth's needs are". By that time, I knew what he meant; but both before then and since, numerous instances have cropped up of spontaneous, instant knowledge regarding "the right thing to do", with plants, with animals, with things, with oneself. It is usually a case, not of realising what needs to be done, but of simply "doing" it. Anything else is not truly instinctive. But in my experience the process never really gets beyond the personal, initial stage. Something happens to block the action, to prevent the ball rolling, almost as though some malicious, destructive force is at work.

Instinctive Solutions not Readily Accepted

This obstructive force, if that is what it is, usually seems to operate through the agency of people – ordinary, fair-minded, well meaning and not at all malicious people – but who (needless perhaps to say) are not themselves motivated by any spontaneous movement from within. Actions which apparently arise from "the soul" are actions which you just *know* are right, and it seems to me that a seemingly unintended but wholly non-instinctive blocking process comes into play as a result. This is hardly surprising, for it is exactly what occurs over the long-term as a normal part of human development. Soul instinct, we could say, is what motivates a new-born child, and is therefore something which we are expected to grow out of. We are *conditioned* to lose it. A very young child is filled with a brand of wisdom quite unknown and unsuspected by adults. As our brains develop, our mind soon discovers that it knows best what it wants, and that it is powerful

11

enough to overrule the instinctual opposition. Parents *encourage* their young child to discard instinctive behaviour and quite unconsciously work to discourage it's return.

Nations are run by the keenest brains, pitting their separate wits one against the other. Whoever heard of a parliament of instinct, or a soul-motivated government? A *religiously* motivated government is not at all the same thing. Plant instinct produces forest and fen; animal instinct produces a rhythmic balance of populations; material instinct holds the whole together and keeps the earth in orbit. All these are linked and interdependent, so much is obvious. But as for human instinct – that was left behind in Eden, the babyhood of humankind. Human brains, as I say, have taken over the function of instinct, and brains are not linked to these basics, these non-thinking processes. Thinking and non-thinking, it seems, just will not mix.

But now I *know* that these two irreconcilables *can* be reconciled, and it has taken me the best part of a lifetime to come to the understanding. Starting from the outcome, looking at the whole question from the standpoint of *soul*, there is nothing to debate, nothing to argue about. But starting from the standpoint of *thought*, the questions, answers and arguments of this day and age seem endless. Brains are never satisfied or willing to stand aside to allow some other faculty to take the stage. Without the modifying influence of instinct, I fear, our clever human brains can be seen as an enemy of the earth!

Natural Instincts of the Non-human World

It is not exactly a "spiritual" thing, this instinct, this *dhyana*; but, as the brain will not allow it to function, it cannot be recaptured in this life (apart perhaps from the odd flash of insight) except through truly spiritual means. Given those means it becomes, as it were, an incidental but wholly necessary bonus to be acquired along the spiritual path. The interlinking of underlying instinct, of things, of plants, of animals, does not leave out the human element.

Brains or no brains, despite our own instincts being set permanently on "hold", these lowly instincts have a powerful effect upon our actions whether we know it or not, but with quite unexpected results.

Perhaps people of the Far East have been more acutely aware than westerners of this spiritual dimension, and in particular of the plant instinct, or plant essence, playing its part in human affairs. There are, for example, the centuries-old crafts of ikebana and bonsai; the theme of both these is concerned with our inner nature. Bonsai, the cultivation of artificially dwarfed trees, could be thought of as an expression of the soul's impoverishment, its frustrated nature; a lament, certainly, for a long-lost human spiritual condition. Ikebana, on the other hand – arranging flowers or vegetation so that they seem in tune with the inner feelings – is expressive of striving. Like bonsai it acknowledges the lowly position at present occupied by the soul, and expresses the desirability of improvement. The implication seems to be that, from the human viewpoint, the plant instincts represent a step *up* in the spiritual order of things.

> Ikebana holds the key
> To appreciating where we stand
> Within the world of wealth: though we seem free
> To hold the pilgrim's latchkey in our hand
> And stay or go at will, manipulate our destiny.
>
> Enslaved by things, materiality,
> In spiritual terms we stand beneath the flowers,
> Caught by the thorns beneath the forest canopy.
> So humble flowers can raise this soul of ours
> Arranged as *shin, soe, hikae,* these three.
>
> *Hikae,* the world, the solid rocky earth,
> And on this world the *soe,* humanity,
> And overhead the path to heaven, new birth
> *Shin* represents the way to immortality
> To stir some memory of the soul's true worth.

The results of both ikebana and bonsai can bring to the observer a calm sense of relief, or peace, a release of tension – something, perhaps, in the nature of confession. Perhaps they offer a window into the unconscious mind, though they cannot by themselves improve anyone's spiritual status, nor can they stir the soul into life. Ikebana arose as an exercise of Zen Buddhism, and is an acknowledgement of the way plants influence people. Zen itself, as may emerge in the course of this book, is the "plant-end" of Buddhism, as opposed to its "material-end". In the past it has seemed to me that Zen Buddhism offered at least a convenient staging post along a journey of inner exploration: a pause for refreshment in my personal (though shared) attempt to find a way back to "the source", via an awareness of and love for the greenery of this planet.

Like that of many others in the past, I believed that my search would have to involve not merely Zen, but traditional Buddhism too, passing to its parent Hinduism, and from Hinduism to its ancestral roots, stripped of its camouflage of ritual, and whatever lay beyond. What lay beyond – that is, in the distant past – may perhaps (or so it seemed to me) prove to be the same as whatever may lie ahead in the problematic future. That mysterious common denominator, I believed, was not religion, not even soul, but Spirit. Christianity has largely freed itself from ancient laws such as the Mosaic prohibitions. A new set of laws, such as that offered by Islam, I for one could well do without. It has become fairly plain that religion without Spirit may be balm for the heart, but can do nothing for the soul.

In my spiritual quest, as I saw it, I would be walking back along a production line, beginning at the end product, such as it is, and ending up at the raw material. The principle would not be one of regression, or diminishing, but of progression to the source, to a rediscovery if not a reoccupation of the spiritual condition symbolised by the Garden of Eden. In no way did I feel that I was somehow betraying the Christianity of my upbringing in the way that many devout Christians do feel, deploring what they may see as dabbling in "eastern religions". On the contrary, exploring such things brought me the realisation, not many years into my journey, that the words of Jesus in his sermon on the Mount, were literally true: "Seek, and ye shall find". To reiterate the point, I have come to realise that religious beliefs, in any case, act solely as comforters for worried emotions, and whatever the mere fact of believing a religious message may or may not have achieved in the past, in this day and age such things cannot serve to awaken the sleeping soul.

Mankind Influenced by the Life Forces of Nature

To any imaginative person, plainly, the spiritual condition of plants, or of animals, does not appear particularly inviting. To people who have experienced them at first hand, these regions of plant and animal instinctual life forces can prove barren and comfortless. The spiritual life forces of materiality, however, the magnetic force of things, minerals, metals, money, the earth itself, when it has influence on human life, is a very attractive proposition indeed – a great source not only of material wealth and comfort, but of wisdom too. It is this materially rewarding life-force that forms the spiritual centre of gravity of the vast majority of people. There they choose to stay, and no wonder. It is good, right and proper for people to be there. But there is one very big "but": all truly spiritual traditions, as well as the teachings of the major religions, have it that this material life force, this so-called *satanic power*, acts on the human soul like a jam jar to a wasp, like birdlime to a bird, flypaper to a fly. This is the most powerful and dangerous aspect the "lower life forces" that hold the soul in bondage to earth and death.

The Soul has a Choice of Directions

My own discovery has been this: if the soul is fortunate enough to receive a vivifying spark, its course may be set in one of two directions: filled with occult experiences, it may plunge deeper into this supernatural zone of materiality, illuminated by the light of Lucifer – a reflection of the light of archangels – shining through the translucent but impenetrable roof, and it will remain bound to earth; or, and far more happily, inspired by the wakened green child within, it may turn its back on the occult, on magic, on reincarnation, on death, and, travelling in the opposite direction, seek the spiritual source.

Starting from the bottom of the heap, the narrow path which leads away from the lure of materiality can only lead upwards through the lower life forces, through the dull but well-regulated realms of plants and animals, through the "ordinary human" realm that we all knew in our childhood but cannot now remember, to the higher human realm and eventually to the light of the higher life forces of seers, sages and saints.

To the scientist unwittingly limited by the brilliance of his own and others' brains; to the philosopher or theorist who, whilst subscribing to the idea of wholeness, cannot help but analyse and in so doing destroys the possibility of wholeness; to the contented follower of an organised religion; or to anyone with a supernatural niche of their own, all this may seem nonsense – even impertinent nonsense. But the comfort of ologies, osophies and isms are not for everyone; and to all those who cannot see a future or find what they need along such well-trodden tracks, I can only stand here among the greenery and point out the lesser known path that leads towards *Susila Budhi Dharma.* No-one can be assured of actually reaching so noble a destination, but each tentative step on this path is surely a step towards a changed and better regulated world.

Let me say now that, as far as I know, the only worldly organisation devoted solely to making this spiritual journey actually possible, is called *Subud* – a contraction of those three Sanskrit words: *Susila, Budhi, Dharma.* There may be other organisations and other ways, I don't know, but I am fairly sure that there are none that do not involve either the use of the will, the desires, or any kind of religious belief. The only requirements are an open mind and a willingness to accept the fruits of one's own experience.

16

The Real Meaning of "Soul"

The true pilgrim on this journey is the soul. It is so easy to speak glibly about "soul". Many people claim to know "soul" when they have in mind something entirely different. But even when it transpires that the speaker or writer who makes confident assertions about "soul" really means "gut-feeling", "conviction", "emotions", or pride in their own cultural background, they are still right in a sense: soul has to contain all these things, and every other driving force as well. But it is only when the inner self really comes to life as a self-contained centre of consciousness, communicating quite independently of thoughts, emotions, and gut-feelings, that one begins to get a little closer to its true meaning. Words and names are mere words and names, but comprehension of this nature grows within those who take a few steps along the path of *Susila Budhi Dharma*.

If someone is searching for soul, they will probably start looking towards religion – perhaps to find a kind of cryptic puzzle where "soul" may again mean "gut-feeling", "conviction", "emotions", or cultural pride. There is no more understand of "soul" within religions or amongst religious people, than anywhere else. Christian missionaries have claimed that they are saving the souls of African pagans, yet in pagan Africa I have found ample evidence of "soul" making itself known almost as a matter of course. It has become obvious to me that soul cannot come to life as a result of any particular ritual, or the pursuit of any particular religion.

Ministers of religion are not stupid, but it sometimes seems that their organisations seem to be claiming the guidance of "Spirit" whilst overlooking "soul" itself – the human part or principle that should surely be open to receive spiritual guidance, and the only human function capable of receiving or communicating with Spirit. This should be what religions and ministers of religion are for: to guide one's soul in the way of Spirit. And yet something seems to be wrong. Standard religions have had a long time to get their act together. Surely, after a few thousand years of supposed spiritual guidance, the world should be running like a well-oiled machine?

Religious Attitudes towards Soul and Spirit

Standard religions may have let us all down, and yet one retains the conviction that somewhere at the root of religion – of all religions – lies the answer we need. Perhaps you, like I, have looked around to see what the various religions have to offer. As Jesus said, "In my Father's house are many mansions", and we usually take that to mean that there is more than one route to spiritual reality (and if you appreciate the symbolism of Christianity, you will understand that "no-one comes to the Father except by me", that is, by way of the personal human soul that has been filled with the Holy Spirit).

But you may discover that these different routes, ways, or religions, though equal in validity and though they believe themselves to be sharing more or less a common goal, are not equal in spiritual content. Not only do the various followers of any particular religion each have his or her individual "level of understanding"; it soon becomes clear that religions themselves have their "levels" – and these levels are not necessarily those with which they started off. Through the combined actions and individual contents of their followers, they have ended up with their own particular centre of gravity, somewhere between the highest and the lowest. And it is the current level of spirituality and understanding within a religion that decides what the common goal of the religious followers is supposed to be; and even when the goal is named, we have once again the free-for-all of definition.

Religious goals are usually a matter of upbringing and cultural background. Those people who seriously adopt a particular religion and pursue it with vigour, are perfectly entitled to their beliefs, and no-one need argue with this. Such beliefs, of course, may be literally true, or symbolically true, or even completely untrue; this is not the point. The point is that religions themselves have a "soul", and the nature of this giant soul corresponds with certain specific aspects of the even greater soul of nature – of Gaia, of Mother Earth herself.

Having said that religions or their adherents believe themselves to be pursuing a common goal, closer inspection is likely to reveal that, from the individual viewpoint at least, there is no common goal to be attained. One man's heaven, it has often been said, is another's hell. Not everyone fits into the moralist's neat black-and-white scheme of life, whether he bids us to "kill!" or to "forgive!". The true "morality" of right living, the *Susila* of *Susila Budhi Dharma*, is a very different level of being, normally unattainable by you or me. Like the way *to* life, it is not a way *of* life that can be won merely by wishing it. When someone is on the right track, this quality arrives and grows within his or her innermost being, without having desired it. In Christian symbolism we can recall the often-misunderstood words of Jesus: *The man who has will be given more; but the man who has not will forfeit even what he has.*

Varying Spiritual "Levels" of Religions

To their devout followers, understandably, all religions are irreproachable. Viewed from the outside, however, purely on a worldly level, even the great world religions, being symbol-based, are fairly full of obvious nonsense. In Christianity, for instance, there is the rather sentimental nonsense of celebrating a virgin birth in practical terms for Jesus, only to ascribe a line of descent for him through his father Joseph. It seems a fairly blatant contradiction, and I am sure no Christian will mind my saying so. The "nonsense" of course arises from the folly of taking symbols as concrete reality, at which point a valuable faith becomes a mere set of beliefs.

Being an older religion, Christianity has largely overcome this particular folly. But one scarcely dare cite examples of symbols being taken as concrete reality from the Islamic tradition,

19

for fear of inciting vengeful reaction – and this simple fact itself reflects a blatant nonsense. It is, however, a highly significant brand of nonsense, for in spiritual terms revenge is a peculiar and unequivocal trait. Revenge does not belong to the material, satanic realms, and people who religiously pursue it may congratulate themselves on that. If the solid matter of materiality is pushed, it stays put, or rolls away, or bounces back, according to its nature, but it has no interest in retribution. Similarly, the animal level of spirituality, to be identified in the life force of the beasts, has no interest in pitting revenge. It crows and roars in victory, or slinks and whines in defeat, but there the matter usually rests. Souls of the true human level, as the lives of saints might show, can perceive too much of their own and others' contents, spiritual and moral, to concern themselves with such pettiness. And as for the creatures of the higher levels of the world of Spirit, having attained spiritual love, I assure you, they are incapable of such behaviour. Revenge lies largely in the province of the plant world, impelled by the natural instincts of plant life: the realm of the *Asuras* of Tibetan Buddhist tradition, the personalised passions of mindless aggression and defensiveness, seen as demons forever warring against the gods and against each other; the realm too of the Green Man of European tradition.

The Influence of Plants on People

People whose souls are taken up by the plant life force are peculiarly volatile, up and down people. Like the actual plants, they may spend their lives in a completely suppressed state, seemingly contentedly so; but they are equally ready to suppress their fellows if they get the slightest chance. Conversely, again like actual plants, they may be quite boundlessly and shamelessly dominant when they achieve the upper hand, accepting only a force greater than their own as a curb for their spread. But because of their up and down nature, they are normally people who do not, in the long term, achieve anything very stable in the world. Like real plants in a real forest, only long term suppression can really achieve permanent stability.

But all this is not the same as to possess any particular feelings, such as sympathy, for the actual plants themselves. Of the world's great religions, only Buddhism, it seems, carries the tradition of trees having significance in the process of enlightenment, and Buddhism alone begins and ends with the concept of aim and effort on the part of humankind as bringing reward, rather than submission to a greater will. Mystical phenomena seem strangely absent within the spiritual world of plants. One could well imagine that the aspirant Buddha's entrance into this abstract plant level could be seen as a step in the ascent to *nirvana*, involving in some measure the cessation of senses and desires. Could it have been significant, I wondered, that the Buddha received his enlightenment whilst seated beneath the bodhi tree, while both his birth and his death took place amidst a grove of sal trees? These trees are quite common in the Buddha's native India: the bo or bodhi tree is a kind of fig, *Ficus religiosa*, and sal is a useful timber tree, *Shorea robusta* (and one which I once planted in Africa on an experimental basis). The implication is that the Buddha was able to draw strength from the bodhi and from the sal by imbibing influences from those trees, and while this may or may not be true for an individual as exalted as the Buddha, it is a useful piece of advice for his followers in the world of nature and materiality.

Spiritual Nature of Plants

As a forester, trees were my main concern. Was the gateway to the spiritual path to be found amongst real trees, I wondered, in the real plant world? Forest religions usually conjure up a vision of nature spirits, of animism. I had already experienced something of the apparent reality of such pagan beliefs, but the nature of such "spirits", I was sure, was somehow less than truly human, and could scarcely be called noble or divine. The great monotheistic religions, Judaism, Christianity, and Islam, all arose, not in well forested areas, but in barren regions, almost as though the spiritual essence of the plant kingdom, having nowhere else to go, began to influence mankind, to enter into the human soul. But of course it could equally well have been the other way round – that the absence of living, breathing plants and their influence somehow opened the way to higher things, to higher influences. The realisation was growing in me that not merely the followers of any particular religion, but people in general were not really quite so "human" as they seemed. On the soul level, could they all be spiritually "animal", "plant", or even "material"?

It seems a truism that only the "true self" can enter the true spiritual path, but this is an important point. When I started "searching" I found I was becoming more and more depressed, at a very deep level. With no apparent outward reason, my depression of the soul lasted for several years. At last the breakthrough came like a flash of light: something was trying to get out, and that something was my own innermost character. I had to accept every part of myself, even the bad parts that I had always thought unacceptable. It was Jung's "shadow" clamouring to be released, and by accepting it I was not shedding it, or becoming overnight a better person. It meant that I had to live with my true nature, warts and all. For the first time, I had become sincere about myself. Everyone has a "persona", a mask which they wear in public, or even in private. But on this spiritual path the soul must lead the whole person: one's "psychology" has to be led, in a way quite contrary to what we have been brought up to believe. The soul must lead, and the soul includes one's whole contents, and not merely the pleasant or socially acceptable parts that you like other people to know about.

Personal "Shadow" and the True Path

This dark "shadow" is not the soul itself, of course, but it is part of its contents. Satan is also a prince in the court of heaven (according to the biblical Book of Job). The soul must lead, and if it is to be accepted as leader, the bad must be accepted along with the good. There is no compulsion to analyse oneself and identify and accept one's own "shadow", no "need" for it; but if you do not accept your own whole nature, good and bad alike, sooner or later the bad bits will make their presence known. In trying to emerge, they will haunt you and hold you back. Soul without Spirit is no more than "contents", but getting to know it and accepting your own contents is a prerequisite if you are to set out on the true path. Particularly religious or moral people may find their own emerging contents unacceptable, and their spiritual progress may prove difficult on this account.

Ironically perhaps, ever-increasing secularism, relaxed moral standards and an "anything goes" culture such as most people in the western world seem to enjoy, would appear to make it easier for ordinary people to find the true path. Few people would notice or comment. Conversely, any sort of return to religious fundamentalism or moral stringency – as we have seen in some other parts of the world – makes it that much more difficult. Strict adherence to religious laws and customs makes even the first step along the spiritual path well-nigh impossible. Westerners in particular who hope to find the true way are not, as a rule, conventionally religious people – certainly not so within the strictures of the great monotheistic religions. "Eastern" religions such as Buddhism and Hinduism in particular, have always tended to respect a personal urge towards spiritual attainment whenever it arises. But in Islam, in Christianity, in Judaism, it has usually been seen as an offence against the order of things for an individual to step outside the strictures of their religious conventions. The age-old complication of mistaking the symbol for concrete reality plays a large part in these religions even today.

Going further, western religious thinking, and in particular the dogma of mainstream Islam, Christianity and Judaism, has tended to identify its own concept of the Ultimate Reality, the person of Almighty God "somewhere out there", with its own ethnic culture, with what it sees as logical social order, and with the moral or even the legal conventions of the day. And so, by somewhat false reasoning, personal infringements of earthly moral or legal restraints have all too frequently been seen as contraventions of divine law.

Religious Convention and the Spiritual Search

To the religious moralist, convention equals purity. But this can be meaningful only on the outside. Who, in their innermost self, is conventional in the sense of "pure"? I doubt if any are truly free from faults and shortcomings, in others' eyes if not their own. Nothing of spiritual significance can happen whilst such faults remain hidden, because they constitute a material burden for the soul. On the other hand, only the spark of divinity can truly clear them out, and as individuals we are helpless. On the face of it, it seems a catch–22 situation. Feelings of guilt are quite inappropriate; we all acquire bad habits during our lives, but other troublesome features may be karmic, inborn, inherited, ingrained, and all are interwoven into the fabric of the soul. Whether one confesses them, like a good Christian, or denies them, like a good Muslim, they are still there just the same. Nobody is perfect. To invent scapegoats, "infidels" to be punished, or saviours outside of oneself, is to approach the concept of the "victim soul":

> Each generation clamouring to be heard,
> each individual racked with problems, self obsessed,
> a situation which has happened since the word
> was first made flesh.
>
> They may not have transgressed
> or perpetrated wrong in their own eyes;
> they may have coped each in their way –
> complaining bitterly,
> or howling their misfortunes to the skies,
> or turning inwards, suffering hardship stoically.
>
> No person relishes the grief of suffering alone,
> though they may wear it as a badge of vanity
> or as a source of pride – at least to make it known,
> and say: 'Why is this burden hoisted onto me
> when troubles of my own would have sufficed?'

Perhaps none else can carry it but them alone.
Yet Christians say: 'Load your burden onto Christ'
as though he hasn't sufferings of his own
enough for two, why should he carry yours?

The father's sins are passed in innocence
down generations, third or fourth,
these are the natural laws.
Are we not responsible for our soul's contents,
or for our bodies with their inherent weakness,
illness, disability, insanity or sin?

Neither Muslim fervour nor Christian meekness
can lose these things:
they merely thrust them deeper in
and lower down, into the depths of their own soul
where they may lie forgotten.

But they live on, disowned by conscious thoughts,
still written on the scroll of life,
until the victim soul can be atoned.
Some may project their burdens and disown them,
loading them across the victim's back,
adding them to the frightful weight
of sin, which people call: to bear a heavy cross.

Such wickedness in innocence contrived
until more and yet more this victim soul
carries the sins of those who died without remission,
which is no longer tenable as many lives unroll.

And comes the time at last to seek submission,
that their souls may be with grace imbued,
and the souls of those who, living, paid the price,
may find redemption through the victim's fortitude,
receivèd into heaven as a holy sacrifice.

Conventional religious thought rarely seems to look
beneath – or should I say above – the level of emotional feeling.
Emotional problems have emotional solutions; but the shedding of

more deeply – or should I say more widely – ingrained faults plainly needs a deeper or wider approach. Familiarity with this deeper or wider level is exactly the quality lacking in civilised society, or so it seems to me. The structure of western religious society in particular seems geared towards creating outsiders: An individual who feels himself or herself to be in conflict with the prevailing social order, for whatever personal reasons, is made to feel that he or she is somehow in conflict with God, at odds with the Ultimate Reality itself.

In practice this means that the only course open to westerners seeking reality in the spiritual field is to abandon – temporarily at least – the standard morality of western religions and look towards the east. Feeling oneself to be in some way "Buddhist" can lend one the freedom to start seeking in earnest, a freedom which is denied mainstream Muslims, Christians, and Jews. To the Buddhist mind, at least as far as I understand it, Almighty God is not conceived as a consciously deliberating, all-seeing, all-judging being who controls the universe, rewarding and punishing on a day-to-day basis. Because divine guidance can operate only through the self, one's innermost self alone has to be the guide. This is not necessarily the *correct* view, but it is a useful temporary staging post. A "healthy agnosticism" can provide a spur to progress.

The Influence of Plant Life on Religious Feeling

Almost by definition, Almighty God is not to be understood. The more one tries to understand, the more one analyses parts, the more one loses sight of the whole. By studying each tree, one can readily overlook the extent of the forest. This is an apt simile for me, because forests have played a major part in my life. As a child and during early adulthood, my affinity seemed to be with the trees, and so did my life and livelihood; from gentle British woodlands to tropical broadleaf and evergreen forest; and in later life an almost endless succession of gardens and landscapes – never to own, but always to feel responsibility for. Having a passion for plants is a way of ensuring that one's soul lives under the influence of the plant kingdom.

How can one best describe the spiritual "plant level" and its influence on humanity? The fierce *Asuras* of Buddhist tradition (of which I shall probably have more to say later) are believed to offer only hostility and strife, and they contrast starkly with the seemingly rather jolly Green Man of European churches. Unbelievable it may seem, but they represent merely a different viewpoint of the same level of spiritual being, and an excellent example of the contrast that exists between extreme aspects of the same life force. It is a contrast that finds its equivalent in the physical attributes of the plant world, with a passive "cabbage" on the one hand, and the overpoweringly rampageous thicket that swamps all opposition, on the other.

Conservation is for "Haves", not for "Have-nots"

Ever since a general concern for the environment became important, it has been rather fashionable to use the image of the Green Man as a symbol of conservation-consciousness, as though he recalls some historical era when humankind was in harmony with nature and Mother Earth. But, in my own understanding, the Green Man was never like that, and nowadays his symbolism is frequently misrepresented. Awareness of the need for conservation grows with the strength not of the plant but of the material life forces – in the outer sense, with the confidence and power that comes with possessions, ownership; with the acquisition and retention of more and more things. It is the "haves" of this world who think conservation or "greenness" a good thing. The "have-nots" tend to find it something of a hurtful jibe. It seems forever to be "getting at" them; yet another stick for the other half of humanity to beat them with.

Television may be sometimes seen as a bane rather than a boon, but it does offer us a glimpse of life in far-away lands, and one thing it has taught us is that rural people in Third World cultures, who barely rub shoulders with that brand of materialism that the wealthier nations take for granted, may seem to be living close to nature, but they are seldom doing so out of respect for their environment, or because of any special understanding of natural resources. Usually, it seems, the case is quite the opposite. In my own experience, people who genuinely live close to nature, from hand to mouth in jungle or desert (and interestingly enough, the two words representing the opposite extremes of success and failure in the plant world apparently have the same Sanskrit root), are only too ready to kill any creature that moves, whether they have a use for it or not, or to cut down a forest tree simply for its fruit, and without a thought of replanting. And when the forest runs out and famine sets in, to tear up the last remaining bush for its fuel. Conservation consciousness becomes formulated as such only when the environment has already lost out, when nature seems to be dying.

"Plant Religion" in Pre-Industrial Times

If we assume that people of the Industrial Age are materially based, and that people of the Agricultural Age, by the same reasoning, are or were plant based in spiritual terms, it follows that people are or were moulded in their relationships towards, on the one hand, material power, and on the other, towards plant power, according to the spiritual nature of these kingdoms. Material subjects, whilst apparently dominating their machines, in practice tend to be dominated by them as slaves of the industrial process. Plant people in their turn have always tended to dominate the real plants whilst remaining completely dependent upon them. This dependence extends into the spiritual sphere too, to such an extent that they also could be called slaves.

Pre-Industrial Revolution people seldom allowed their plants to grow as nature had intended. Their trees for instance rarely reached their natural proportions, but found themselves brutally curtailed, lopped, topped, brashed and debarked, providing building materials, fuel, fodder, tannin and sometimes medicine and food, and valued only for their produce. The whole countryside was one vast factory, and plants which could not be put to use were suppressed. "Coppice with standards", for instance – the ancient system of broadleaf forestry very much in favour with modern environmentalists as supportive of wildlife – is entirely a factory system, supplying the bark for leather-tanning as well as rods, timber, fuel and fodder.

This was the working environment presided over by the Green Man, as depicted in many a village church, composed of vegetation as though to symbolise his willingness to supply human needs. In a sense this could be called a state of greenness within – the spiritual level of plant life occupying the centre of gravity within the collective human soul, with humans at the top of the tree, themselves overgrowing and suppressing all other vegetation, all other life forms, to serve their own nutritional needs.

In pre-Christian days of "plant religion", sacred groves existed in stark contrast with the thoroughly exploited everyday vegetation. By definition sacred groves were special preserves, needing special managers with official powers of enforcement. The point I would like to make is that these managers – these priests of the sacred groves – were probably not themselves plant-level people. Like King Solomon, so much more wise, wealthy and powerful than his people, the custodians of a plant-level religion would have to be of a *material* level themselves (like the general run of people today). A seeming paradox, for priests are bound to be seen by their followers, the religious masses, as occupying a higher spiritual niche than themselves. It was the ordinary lay folk who came to worship at these sacred groves (or, as it may be, who were excluded from them) who were the real plant-force people in that they were largely limited to that spiritual centre of gravity.

According to anthropologists, the belief in "crop spirits" is or has been fairly universal. But in the days before people began to grow crops, spiritual allegiance was offered not to the plants, but to the animals – before human closeness to and reliance on the animal world began to diminish. As a process, this spiritual descent is only now drawing to its conclusion. I have seen it and felt the effects of it, like a rickety old ladder still in use despite its missing rungs, still taking place in parts of Africa.

Religious Development seen as Spiritual Decay

The fact is, religion starts high and develops downwards, though it may seem to us to be developing from primitive roots to an ever-increasing level of sophistication. From the original human level (before the time of Abraham, perhaps) it has descended, through the animal-based totemic and shamanic religions, from the worlds of Pan and Cernunnos, through sacred groves and along avenues of magnificent, revered trees which gradually gave way to the wonderful towering stone trees represented in the tracery of Gothic cathedrals. And still down and down, from the world of children through to adulthood, parallel religious development has led deeper and deeper into corresponding spiritual decay. But when something miraculous can intervene to halt the downward spiral and allow spiritual development to begin, when the slow process of purification of the soul can commence, everything shifts into reverse gear. From barren maturity we can climb back up the hill, degree by degree, until we are able to become again like little children.

From BIRTH: ....*Human*

Animal

Plant

To MATURITY: ....*Material*

This, I submit, is the real barrier between the spiritual and the material, as far as normal life on earth is concerned: not the innocence of a newborn child, not the dizzy heights of the saintly higher human level, but the actual base of materiality, the boundary line, to cross which leads, in one direction, to the realm of Satan (implying familiarity with wealth and welfare, possessions and power), and in the other direction to the realm of the Green Man. In material terms, the realm of the Green man may be seen as a place of luxurious growth; in spiritual terms it may be seen as a desert, and in its higher reaches certainly, a place wherein luxury, luck, success in business and a good standard of living, may all cease to function.

By becoming centred in the plant level, one is in a sense that much closer to nature, but certainly that much "farther from the earth". Newcomers to this zone may find that they have arrived in a far larger sphere of being than the material zone with which we have become so familiar. Spirituality in the mystical sense may seem to be lacking, but this sphere in fact represents a far higher spiritual state than that of the everyday Tom, Dick, and Harry who normally inhabit our world. Perhaps this is one reason why some plant-based drugs can prove so addictive, seemingly offering a psychic expansion, an experience instinctively seen as that much closer to heaven.

Symbolism of the Green Man

When we determine to climb out of the spiritual zone of materiality there is really only one way to go: and whether we see our goal as approaching an impersonal Green Man as representative of the spiritual plant kingdom, or more personally as embracing an innocent green child representing our own inner self; whether we see our goal in terms of the world or in terms of ourselves, makes no difference in the long term. To seek the one implies the discovery of the other, for in order to grow and expand from the material level one needs to experience that rebirth symbolised by the green child within. To progress from the rock-bottom level of materiality towards the source, entails invasion of the Green Man's territory.

The enigmatic Green Man:
> god-demon poised midway twixt heaven and hell
> shunning companions, lacking family or wife,
> there is no green woman of whom fables tell,
> his alone is the symbol of nature-bound life.

He guards the span,
> the breach between two world-cleaving themes,
> the one, of goddesses, gods, and time:
> the other, a path of escape which redeems
> our lives, above nature's mantle: a power divine.

The pagan perception
> of flourishing, fruiting, dying, rebirth,
> flesh reincarnated again and again,
> a vegetal status for people of earth:
> the cycling seasons – no loss, and no gain.

The prophetic inception
> of great world religions and new understanding,
> the hope of rebirth into some higher state,
> a chance to escape this perpetual recycling,
> redeemed, and assured of the conquest of fate.

The watchful Green Man
> holds a major concern for the welfare of man,
> for our birthright was squandered or sold to the devil
> through the gamut of life from when humans began –
> and his power is affirmed over souls of *plant* level.

This god-demon stands
> as though guarding the gateway to some lonely track
> through the forest. Below: power, riches and fame;
> young souls seek acclaim and the power that they lack;
> old souls feel the need to ascend whence they came.

Both ways he commands:
> overhead is a path that's called narrow and straight;
> we are loath to ascend this inscrutable course,
> but the urgings of soul and the promptings of fate
> both point to the Way that leads back to the Source.

There are quite a number of European legends depicting the Green Man as a person, a type of giant, or a well-meaning ogre (like the Green Knight who rode into King Arthur's court). If the common spiritual route of humankind entails a growing-away from an original state of closeness to God, with the accompanying ever-increasing development of mental powers and strength of emotions, it seems to me that legends such as these suggest a process of backtracking. They represent an invitation or a desire to climb back through unconsciously shed layers of spirituality. Perhaps this is why the Green Man is so often to be seen depicted in Christian places of worship.

The household tales of some lands feature proverbial giant-killer Jack's encounters with the Green Man. There is usually some sort of game to play, some kind of gamble or challenge to be accepted; but it operates only if Jack has gold, or the wherewithal to gamble. If, that is, he is already in possession of the wealth and power that only materiality can bestow, and if he is willing to risk sacrificing this in order to climb back through the spiritually unrewarding level of the plants. The world's wealth is obtainable only at the ultimate material depth, if not deep in the earth itself, where it is guarded by kobolds and gnomes. Perhaps, just perhaps, Jack may succeed in carrying some of this wealth, and more besides, back "home". This is the gamble, and this is the challenge.

Experiencing Spiritual Levels

All this, I readily admit, is not really a matter to concern the intellect. But imprecision is inevitable, for the analytical mind cannot begin even to identify levels of spiritual being. Perhaps it is just as well that I personally am not an intellectual person. My usual centre of gravity is very much an emotional one, and I can only hope that I do not exasperate the intelligent reader with my woolly thinking. But the fact is that "spiritual levels" are neither intellectual nor emotional. Neither heart nor mind are appropriate vehicles with which even to approach the intangible world of spirit, even on so lowly a level as that of the plants. Neither heart nor mind are able by themselves to find a suitable path. But it is not always necessary to understand a problem in order to apprehend it; direct experience may override both thoughts and feelings, and bring understanding in its wake.

If you walk where I have walked you may discover a kind of thinking that is not apparently connected with the intellect, and a kind of feeling that is not apparently connected with the emotions. Perhaps this was the sort of thing referred to by Georges Gurdjieff when he spoke of "higher centres" – or perhaps not. But on my own very humble level I can assure you, if you do not already know it, that clever brains and sensitive hearts can achieve nothing of use on this spiritual plane. There is a world of difference, too, between *any* preconceptions you may have already entertained about this state of affairs, and your own ongoing wholly practical experiences when they occur.

To accept the principle of greenness into one's inner life, in this sense, entails sacrifice – a voluntary state of quite involuntary sacrifice – because the act of turning one's back on the metaphorical valley abyss of materiality involves the probability at least of losing out on worldly wealth. The wealthier and more fortunate one is to start with, the harder it will seem. It is not quite like the case of the wealthy man who, after receiving advice from Jesus to sell everything he had and give the proceeds away, could not bring himself to part with his wealth (prompting Jesus to remark that it was easier for a camel to pass through the eye of a needle, than for a rich man to enter the Kingdom of Heaven). It is easier for us, because it is not a voluntary giving up of anything; it happens of its own accord. It is not really a matter of wealth; it is a matter of our *attachment* to the material, and the necessity for breaking that spiritual attachment which tends to holds us down like a ghost in chains. I have seen it again and again, happening to those who no longer wish to serve the material life forces (and who remain, needless to say, quite unable to control those forces). It becomes time to "consider the lilies of the field", the rising from the ground level of materiality to the level of the plant forces.

Like the biblical patriarch Job, one will find oneself tempted by Satan. Tempted not *with* an extra something held out as a bribe, but by a withholding of the benefits of materiality; by a *withdrawing* of worldly success and security so that your very existence seems barren. A temporary state it may be, but its duration in each case is unknown and cannot meaningfully be forecast. In this strange condition, as though fallen between two stools, your best efforts may seem to come to nought; there can be no assurance. Other people, still steeped in materiality themselves, are induced to work against you. One can do little but hope that fortune will be restored when God wills. There can be no turning back; the bond between yourself and the power of materiality must be broken, and this will be its own proof that progress is real. One can only accept it in faith.

Spiritual Characteristics of Animals

If we are looking back up the spiritual hill down which we have come to reach adulthood, we can see that the level above that of the plants is the animal realm. Sooner or later this too must be entered and explored. If ancient Buddhism can be instrumental in allowing entry into the plant realm, it follows that the far more ancient Hindu religion should offer an insight into this spiritual kingdom of the beasts. The Hindu culture is well filled with both plant and animal influences, a religion of images: of animal-force gods and goddesses; of discarded garlands supplementing the diet of holy cows in the streets of Benares.

People of the plant level, it seems to me, possess a strongly hierarchical view of animals. To a man of the truly human spiritual level, an animal is an animal in purely realistic terms; to a man of the material level, an animal may be seen in equally realistic terms, but it may also be given a special emotional status. But to a person whose spiritual level is somewhere in between the human and the material, every creature may be ascribed a spiritual rank, ranging from the high to the low. A few animals seem to be particularly respected in traditional Far Eastern society, though such respect bears little relationship to the reality of "animal levels" as seen from the inside, but rather its reflection as a folk-memory. There is the often-tamed elephant – seen perhaps as the animal shape of humanity and the epitome of worldly wisdom; the tiger – a "real" animal in its own right, and overlord of the jungle; the often-domesticated buffalo – a real "animal's animal"; the holy cow – an animal that lives on the spiritual level of materiality, hence its revered or semi-revered status; and the rhino – an animal of the plant world, if ever there was one, an *Asura* of an animal.

It is perhaps little wonder that the rhino should have become so potent a symbol of self-sufficiency. Favouring the more remote areas of dense, swampy, jungly country near the northern mountains, and despite its inevitable and increasing vulnerability in these pragmatic times (unlike its poacher-persecuted African cousins which inhabit dry, open woodland, and have never inspired such thoughts, as far as I am aware, amongst African peoples), the great Indian rhinoceros, with its majestic bulk, afraid of nothing, unhurried and seemingly without desires, browsing peacefully in the thicket – the possessor too of that magic horn – this silent creature has always impressed the local human populace with its aura of aloof independence. Because of its solitary nature, the Indian rhinoceros used to be seen as a sort of role model for serious Buddhist behaviour, as this, my transliteration of the ancient poem "Behold the Rhino" suggests. It was originally intended for the guidance of Buddhist monks, and it certainly predates Zen:

Judge not thy fellow creature, man,
And other creatures harm thou none.
Seek not approval for thy plan;
Behold the rhino: walk alone.

A true companion of like mind
Can seek together to atone.
But friends like this are hard to find,
Behold the rhino: walk alone.

Thus longs the heart – a heavy chain,
So do not seek a friend; a son.
The bonds of love can prove a bane,
Behold the rhino: walk alone.

A tangled thicket blocks the way;
A chainèd heart impedes a man.
The air is free where tree tops sway.
Behold the rhino: walk alone

Thus be content, without desire
Envy and malice bear thou none.
Passions make all-consuming fire.
Behold the rhino: walk alone.

Wild creatures of the forest free,
They have no hamp'ring need for home.
So man, with passions gone, can be;
Behold the rhino: walk alone.

Till greed, and grudge, and guileful schemes,
Till all delusions, faults, are gone,
Till world's desires seem nought but dreams,
Behold the rhino: walk alone.

When noble truth o'ercomes all fears,
And points the sure path hardly won,
At last the inner guide appears!
Behold the rhino: walk alone.

Ancient Guidance for Buddhist Monks

Probably the vast majority of men and women of all religions or
none find social relationships compellingly desirable, and perhaps
poems like this one helped to soothe the aspirant monk's obligation
to forgo such perfectly natural desires. Obviously its message is
one of self-sufficiency, and also of celibacy – a principle that
reappears in accounts of early Christian communities and has
significance for Catholics today. As a lifelong bachelor myself, I
felt it incumbent on me to find out, if only out of interest, and

purely for my own benefit, whether a state of celibacy is indeed a help, or a hindrance, along the spiritual path and the quest for greenness.

Ancient Guidance for Christian Disciples

The person responsible for more of the Bible than any other single author was probably St Paul, and so when comparing the varying attitudes towards society that have been recommended by the founding fathers of the world's main religions, his advice on celibacy and lust can scarcely be ignored. It seems likely that Christ's own celibate example persuaded Paul that the life of a disciple would be set that much more firmly on the true spiritual path by forgoing marriage, and the social conventions of common men. But celibacy was never recommended for the ordinary followers either of Buddhism or of Christianity.

To me, St Paul represented (and in many ways still represents) the "Buddhist side" of Christianity. The "Islamic side" of Christianity, like Islam itself, has never so much as considered celibacy as a possibility. To the much married Prophet Mohammed; even to Pak Subuh Sumohadiwidjojo, and to most of their respective followers, the desirability of marriage from every standpoint has seemed self-evident. If intellectual arguments can be made for celibacy, even stronger arguments can be made to the contrary. In all ages, and perhaps now as never before, rather than a celibate hierarchy (who never advocated celibacy for the masses) it has been the married men themselves who advocate marriage as an essential adjunct to the spiritual path, and who insist on the superiority of their marital status over bachelorhood or celibacy.

Seeking Spiritual Guidance for Today

So who is closer to "the way" – the dedicated loner, or the ever-occupied family man? Well, you may say, not everyone (and more likely, very few indeed) *can* be celibate, or self-sufficient; and not everyone *can* be married, or sociable. If one is seeking sound guidance, that guidance cannot reasonably be expected to come from the common base of humanity, who may or may not seek, but who would all like to find the best way to climb. All guidance is questionable when it comes from some smug Jack who is all right. And certainly experience shows that nothing of value can come from man's pride in his own ability to climb, whether aided or unaided. The answer to any question concerning a spiritual path, a spiritual goal, to be of an spiritual value, must come from the spiritual source itself. This spiritual source itself will guide the individual in such matters.

It seems self-evident, and all religions seem to confirm, that neither a keen mind (or a woolly one), nor a passionate heart (or a cold one) can find the way. From our earthly viewpoint with its narrow horizons, to borrow Gurdjieff's classification of human types, neither a monk nor a householder, whatever his personal views, marital status or moral rectitude, is able by taking thought even to approach the path. It is the path that has the means to approach the man. Man can seek in vain, because it is not he who chooses. In the words of the Upanishads, "Spirit seeks, and Spirit chooses". Man, at best, can only accept, or reject.

If one approaches *Subud* for the opening of the soul, it soon becomes evident that the previous pursuit of *dhyana,* which for so long has seemed quite important, gives way without any conscious intent to the pursuit of *dharma,* and the establishment of something far more "spiritual" than mere instinct. Technique must give way unequivocally to a whole new way of life.To recapture basic human instincts has to entail no less than a coming to life of the soul; a shaking off of the trammels of materiality. The "self" simply cannot be relied upon to lead and find the path; one must lay oneself open to the guiding Spirit. One may have adopted a Buddhist viewpoint in order to breach the barrier of contradiction between right and wrong, can and can't, but sooner or later one will be constrained to return to a strictly monotheistic concept of a single, all-seeing, all-loving God. To do less is to invite further fragmentation which can only disrupt the search for wholeness.

Ancient Legends Offering Clues

To travel back in time searching for records of truly "human" people and their origin is to cross the boundary from literal history into myth. The legend of Adam and Eve, and similar stories about the origins of humanity, recur with numerous variations in different cultures throughout the world. An original blissful state is followed by expulsion or demotion from this state with the growth of worldly knowledge. And of course it was not merely curiosity about the evolutionary physical origin of a human species that inspired these legends. Chiefly they reflect an inbuilt instinctive awareness that humankind here on earth somehow occupies a central place in the celestial order of things, poised midway, as it were, between heaven and hell. And, in my view, they make it plain that deliberate intentions and mere determination to succeed, are completely out of place in any spiritual search.

The human soul
– the subtle self –
with or without religious rote
is set between the two extremes
of heaven and hell,
the high and low.

And both extremes
are great unknowns:
the soul may rise or fall
– untrammelled lightness
or full-laden gravity –
conflicting influence.

But influences for the soul
must pull and draw
they cannot push away,
and those below the human soul
determined, passionate,
pull down to gravity.

Determination, fervour,
act as anchors to the soul:
when influences flow
from sources higher than our own,
childlike submission
lifts the soul to heaven.

In the spirit of *Sahid Anwar* and *Sahid Anwas*, some of the most outstanding human characteristics, or strengths and weaknesses – and particularly those traits that seemed to the legend spinners most strongly to divide humanity into opposing camps – have been ascribed to the sons and daughters of Adam, or his equivalent as the father figure of mankind. They stress the fundamentally different approaches to life and to religion that have characterised what may be seen as two distinct lines of descent spanning millennia, and these cultural differences have overridden even the gradual separation of the human race into its varied ethnic groups. Thus within any race we can find two distinct approaches to matters of religion, matters of faith.

Most creation traditions include an original father figure – the truly human one who marked the end of a spiritual-human universal state, and the beginning of ordinary humankind; Adam, shall we say, forced to live on earth in material form with a thinking, analysing mind and a feeling, judging heart, able to tell the difference between right and wrong. According to the Book of Genesis it was Adam's eldest son, Cain, tiller of the soil, who murdered his brother Abel, keeper of sheep. It would seem more likely in the dawn of humanity that Abel was a hunter rather than a sheep farmer, but in any case it illustrates the beginning of a natural sequence: the descent from the pristine human condition, through animal and plant levels of soul being, finally to arrive at a spiritual relationship or familiarity with the benefits of materiality. Hunter-gatherers may follow their instincts, but farming is a sophistication, a development not of instinct but of free will. Adam himself was a human-oriented person; Abel was an animal-oriented person; Cain was a plant-oriented person, and like certain plant-oriented people of the present day (slash-and-burn peasants, for example) his lot was to roam the land like wind-blown seed, putting down roots where he could.

Cain, as a child growing, or descending, from the equivalent human state of babyhood, being the eldest, had descended further than Abel and, having reached the fierce plant level, finally put paid to the animal state by symbolically murdering his younger brother. Abel, if you like, was a younger version of Cain, whom he had killed simply by growing out of his own childhood.

The Great Divide : Conflicting Attitudes

To return to the Javan version of the conflict between Adam's sons, which of course tells a different story: the characters this time of course are *Sahid Anwar* and his brother *Sahid Anwas*. The story relates how *Anwar* was an obedient child, humble and submissive to divine order, and compliant in following both his father Adam's bidding and the Creator's will. His brother *Anwas* was the very opposite: not wicked or criminal like his Judaic counterpart, Cain, but obstinate, self-willed, and determined to make the world run the way he wanted. For him, Eden was a state to be regained and, if necessary, to be taken by storm. This story, it seems to me, sheds further significant light on all that has happened over the centuries, regarding people's attitudes to spiritual matters. The difference is very much alive today.

The brothers *Anwar* and *Anwas*, we could say, were second generation immigrants to the world of materiality and pioneers of the human immersion into the instinctual world of nature. With the death of Adam and Eve any personal memory of the artless state of Eden had already gone, and gradually the folk memory too began to fade from human minds. We can imagine that every man, not yet too heavily steeped in materiality to have forgotten completely, would construct his own picture of the blissful conditions to which he hoped he might one day return. But to complicate matters he had inherited one of the two distinctive personal attitudes towards that image and that desire. Totally imaginary and mythical though the story is, the principle is still readily observable today. The two incompatible attitudes of *Anwas* and *Anwar* which resulted in two distinct directions of racial or cultural approach towards spiritual matters, handed down through the ages, represents a deep rift which has shown itself in our conflicting attitudes towards religion throughout the ages, and probably in our approach to the more practical matters of conservation too.

Direct Action, or Humble Submission?

Though seldom recognised for what it is, the schism is as deep and wide today as it has ever been, dividing individuals and races. As a principle, *Anwar* represents those religions (in their original forms at least) and religious attitudes both ancient and modern, by means of which their adherents hope or hoped to return one day to the blissful state through humble submission to the will of God, as they understand it, if by no other means than by following the teachings of successive prophets and divine messengers.

Those who represent the attitudes of *Anwas*, on the other hand, typically profess allegiance to religious or philosophical systems which recommend direct action as a means of regaining a state of bliss, through a process of creating or strengthening a hidden side of their nature by concentrating the passions, directing the will and commanding the mind, through the practice of self discipline. As representatives of the *Anwas* line of descent we could say that human-form gods such as Zeus or Jupiter arose as though to personify what was seen as the pinnacle of man's unaided achievement.

Probably most of the ancient civilisations such as the Roman, the Babylonian, the Chinese, and the Egyptian were very much *Anwas* by nature, and King Solomon stands out as an *Anwas* achiever within the Judaic tradition. Amongst world religions today, *Anwas* is typified, not merely by Buddhism, but also by various sects belonging to other major religions, by yoga and magic, by numerous New Age cults and attitudes, and any other system or "way" which has as its aim the achievement of some kind of spiritual strength or supernatural power through work on oneself. Conversely, *Anwar* is typified by the great monotheistic religions – when these are conducted in the submissive spirit recommended by their respective founders.

This is the great and important divide, a fork in the track that few even notice exists. *Anwas* strives to breach the outer self in order to attain the Buddha-self within. *Anwar* submits all progress to the will of God, and thereby invites the inner self to make its presence known. Both are agreed that the passions – the ceaseless functioning of all the cares, desires, hopes and fears of this world – are the stuff of the outer self and the barrier to higher things. Both attitudes seek to nullify the effect of these passions. *Sahid Anwas* in effect operates from the sensual outside and works inwards. *Sahid Anwar* does not and cannot "operate" at all; he can only wait patiently, in hopeful expectation for the process to begin by itself through the ingress of Spirit, and from the inside work its way outwards.

The 7th century Chinese "Song of the Tao" hints at this contact with Spirit, and sums up the duality of this step along the path to Ultimate Reality:

> Like empty space it has no bounds,
> Yet it is there, profound and clear.
> Yearning, you grasp at empty space,
> Too far to comprehend – too near!
> Then understand you know it not.
> In knowing not, you find this place.
> When you are silent, still, it speaks –
> But then you speak, and find but space.
> Yet it is there, smells, sights and sounds,
> The open gate, profound and clear.

Four Ways, and a Fifth Way?

Ancient writings such as this offered me a tantalising glimpse of possibilities which I knew lay somewhere ahead. Before fully appreciating the difference between the attitudes of *Anwas* and *Anwar*, I had been following that remarkable system of self advancement taught by Georges Gurdjieff and known as the "Fourth Way". As Gurdjieff himself put it, it offered the best one could do the "pass the time" until death. It was acknowledged to be a transitional stage, and even its successful completion could be no more than a temporary measure, until the arrival of a speculated "Fifth Way" that should be able to lift mankind over the hurdle which he knew existed – the achievement of positive contact with the soul, the centre of personal spiritual growth.

The "Fourth Way" followed in natural sequence from the so-called "First Way" of the fakir, the "Second Way" of the monk, and the "Third Way", that of the yogi. Rising above these three ways, the Fourth Way could be called the "way of the householder" – that is, of the ordinary, responsible person. But it was also the way of *Sahid Anwas*, and its completion would represent the pinnacle of man's inner achievement by use of the will.

5th Way	Submission to higher influences	?
4th Way	Work on consciousness	Limit of *Sahid Anwas*
3rd Way	Work on the mind	Limit of the yogi
2nd Way	Work on the feelings	Limit of the monk
1st Way	Work on the body	Limit of the fakir

It was a fascinating system (and though I tried to follow it diligently for several years, it is a relief in no pejorative sense to speak of it now in the past tense) in which no withdrawal from everyday life was needed. It was aimed at achieving an individual understanding and at least partial control of the complicated human organism by analysing its functions and centring its awareness. By pursuing this work, and reducing the multiplicity of "I's" to a single "I", it was hoped to create a "deputy steward" to manage the human household until such time as the real steward arrived. His arrival would represent a crossing-over to higher things – to the additional arrival perhaps, of the real but unknown lord of the household.

A Finer than Human Agency

Such higher possibilities would have to depend upon the intervention of a then unknown man who had somehow gained a higher standing in the spiritual hierarchy. A halfway point in the universal order of things, above worldly nature but below that of the angels, has to be the upper limit to which a mortal man can aspire without the help of some finer-than-human agency, and to be open to the influence of this fine agency is to be open to submissive faith.

If Gurdjieff's Fourth Way was the pursuit of soul, the First Way, the way of the fakir, would have to involve mastering the physical body and overpowering the sensations by concentrating them in one prolonged effort. The Second Way, the way of the monk, would have to involve conquering the heart, channelling the emotions through constant prayer, and overriding physical considerations by way of unquestioning obedience to religious dogma. The Third Way, the way of the yogi, would have to involve work on the mind, developing the power of concentration and, overriding both emotional and physical considerations, focusing pure thought on a narrow objective.

Of these three ways I am quite sure that the way of the fakir is the most difficult one to follow, and its results probably the most dubious in value. The monk's path, I am also sure, is a difficult one to tread sincerely, and its outcome too is uncertain. A yogi (in the fullest meaning of the word) needs to work constantly on his mind, and even if wholly successful his only possible future

ZEN AND THE GREEN MAN

is finally to lose his intellectual strength and everything he has gained, in death. The "householder" pursuing the Fourth Way whilst going about his normal everyday affairs may find the practice less arduous, and the results more enduring than those of the preceding ways, but he still cannot progress beyond the material sphere of influence. Its value may even be negative: its successful completion will have involved the creation of an "artificial soul", which may eventually prove an unwanted burden. The true soul meanwhile will remain unaltered.

Ancient Hindu Advice on Seeking a True Teacher

This is the point where the need for some sort of guru is most keenly felt. If you are like me, however, you will harbour a powerful mistrust of gurus, and, I still think, rightly so. At this stage we need something much more, much higher than mere words and theories, higher even than excursions into occult realms. The Hindu Upanishads described exactly the kind of guru or teacher needed, and the truth of this is the same now as it was two thousand years ago:

Our minds are in confusion over matters of the soul because of the endless contradictions of our teachers — because of the imperfection of words.

True teachers are not those well versed in sacred books. True teachers are those who have contact with eternity through Spirit. To the pupil who approaches such a teacher with mind and heart at peace, is opened the way to Spirit.

Whom the sages call teacher is one possessed by Spirit. The wise man who stills his thoughts and desires in the presence of such a teacher attains Spirit. Meditation is the lamp that lights this truth.

And I might add, experience is an even more reliable lamp to light this truth. I hope that the conviction will grow in you as it did in me, if you have been following a way typical of *Sahid Anwas*, that further progress, if it is to be meaningful, must take

47

place along some other route; in practical terms, it must be totally personal, and it must therefore involve submission, not to rules or dictats, but to one's own higher self. Having realised the inadequacy of heart and mind when faced with the problem of discovering one's own higher self, one cannot help but feel that traditional channels of the *Anwar* type also fail to provide the needed guidance. Their premises and aims may indeed seem irrelevant. Religions may seem to hold out quite inappropriate hopes. It becomes obvious that life of the Spirit and "religion" are not at all the same thing.

The Path of Susila Budhi Dharma

One's own progress along the path of enlightenment may be compared with speculative human progress after death. It seems unlikely that spiritual progress, whether before or after death, could depend upon the *will*, which regularly disappears even during sleep. It must depend solely upon that Spirit which remains untouched by desiring, even though its acceptance requires simple belief. Even great minds – or perhaps, *especially* great minds – do not always appreciate the difference between the twin attitudes of *Anwas* and *Anwar*. Strength of mind may even be a disadvantage; perhaps one must be prepared to be more like the old man in the *Punch* cartoon, who "sometimes sits and thinks, and sometimes just sits". Even if *Sahid Anwas* reaches the pinnacle of achievement, the true path of *Susila Budhi Dharma* is not even begun. The early promptings of *dhyana* always suggested that the gateway to that path lay in the direction of the Green Man and his kingdom, through that tangled web of natural but non-human instincts.

One of the finer points of the Fourth Way was that it allowed at least a possibility of developing the truly human passion of "not wanting" – a "non-passionate" passion that leaned towards *Anwar*, although the system itself was still one hundred percent an *Anwas* way. It was this possibility that allowed a few of Gurdjieff's followers, some ten years after his death, to move away from the principle of *Anwas* to that of *Anwar*; towards what they perceived as a possible "fifth way"; towards contact, in fact, with Pak Subuh Sumohadiwidjojo.

A major problem faced by an *Anwas* personality when changing horses in midstream is the difficulty of accepting basic humble simplicity as a desirable state, and a prerequisite for entering the way of submission. For such a personality, simplicity has never been a starting point; it was always an extra state of mind, something that must be painstakingly created and preserved. It is not easy to become again like a little child. It is no easier in the East. To the Buddhist intellectual, certainly, there is only one simple reality, though countless lives have been dedicated and millions of words written to demonstrate this lack of complication. In whatever language, the way to Ultimate Reality, though simple in itself, cannot be recognised with ease. Awakening to simplicity is a long-term process.

Possibilities of Zen as a "Plant Religion"

I have already mentioned how my musing on the spiritual aspects of the plant kingdom led me to study the possibilities raised by ikebana, and this in turn led to its inspirational fount, Zen Buddhism. Approached from a slightly different angle such a connection would not of course be apparent, but to me it seemed perfectly plain that Zen is essentially a "plant religion". Its essential driving passion, again it seemed to me, is that of the spiritual life forces of the plant world – what we might call the sum total of plant instincts. The possessiveness of materiality, and the rituals of the animal life force are both scorned by Zen devotees. With its "non-striving aims" Zen is a transitional phase between *Anwas* and *Anwar*, or so once again it seems to me, a state between the purposeful search for enlightenment, which in retrospect I know to be the wrong approach, and the setting aside of "attitude", the suspension of thoughts and feelings, and the trusting submission of "I" to a non-passionate, non-personal, "non-I". But never for one moment should you think that Zen is the fifth way.

49

If we must look with our tidy minds for neat starting and finishing points, I suppose Zen could be said to commence within the *Anwas* mind at that point where the everyday conceptual self-improving "self" ceases to make progress in spiritual terms. Having finally achieved enlightenment, or what Buddhists call *satori*, at the point where Zen has nothing further to gain or seek, there, at the entry of *Anwar*, we might expect to find the commencement of *Susila Budhi Dharma*. It was this completely unknown state that had to be the fifth way – a way of life that follows the awakening of truly human consciousness.

Direct Action Without "Will"

From *Anwas* to *Anwar*: it seems a small and subtle change of perception. For any sincere man or woman of any religion or none, in theory, nothing could be simpler. "Spirit is not sought", say the Upanishads, "Spirit seeks". All that is required, it seems, is patient acceptance, a feeling of *humble* submission, a feeling, not that "We are gods!" or even the emotional "I believe; I am saved!" but rather an acknowledgment as in the Revelation of St John, that: "I am poor, and blind, and naked". It constitutes the withdrawal of pride in will.

In the world of commerce and society, of course, the will has to be operative. If you try to "submit" or "receive" your way through the workaday world, nothing gets done. In this respect the path is narrow and difficult to tread. There is no exact route map. Like the Pilgrim's Progress, it is a way of compromise, a continual adjustment to changing circumstances. The old gibe aimed by politicians at their opponents, that they have "no coherent policy", or that they seem to be playing everything by ear, can be seen as an expression of approval. Spontaneity and sincerity are crucial, but one cannot really strive for spontaneity without losing it; equally one cannot be intentionally sincere without sacrificing sincerity. As Zen masters say: "You cannot find it by taking thought; you cannot find it by not taking thought".

It is also said in Zen: if a seed is to germinate and develop into a tree, it simply needs to grow. If a fish is to evolve and get anywhere at all, it simply needs to swim. If a bird is to progress, it simply needs to fly. The seed that first must learn how to analyse the soil, the fish that first has to feel the need to discover the extent and nature of the water, and the bird that first must examine the extent and nature of the sky, will never get anywhere. This is an expression of direct action as a living need. If you have the idea of searching for improvement, you are already working *against* true attainment. A 6th century patriarch expressed his Zen "faith" in this verse:

> By following your nature you follow the Way;
>> Make your way leisurely, quieten the mind.
> Worries and puzzlements shut out reality;
>> Fight not the passions; let them unwind.

Chasing Symbols

The same principle has been expressed in many differing cultures: "It is an error not to seek God; but it is also an error to seek God, for God is already closer to oneself than one's own self." Such a conclusion seems inevitable when we take the view that creation is already with us, that Spirit is already here, that God is already omnipresent. We can only "seek" some finite goal, something detached from ourselves and our lives. To seek in this material sense is to create a symbol outside of the self, and then to chase after that symbol.

Almighty God almost by definition is impersonal and not to be sought. "God the Personal", however brought about, whatever catalyst is needed to change theory to the reality of experience, can only be a part, or potential part or principle, of one's own self. To "know God" is to become aware of this aspect, this spiritual constituent of the self. The catalyst will certainly have a collective, impersonal nature: but the experience itself and all that ensues must be wholly personal.

Many in Zen have carried this fairly obvious conclusion a stage too far and maintained: "I have no other self but the experience, the knowledge, the total of my awareness. There is no distinction between me and the things of which I am aware. I am all. I walk alone." Such thinking seems to carry us back to the beginning, to the lonely rhino of the Buddhist poem. But in the spiritual-plant world where Zen lives, loners do not really get on. Aloneness on that particular plane implies a fortress-like state of invincibility, or touch-me-not sensitivity. Nobody wants to be as lonely as the Javanese Upas tree (not wholly mythical but an actual tree with poisonous sap – *Antiaris toxicaria,* which is quite untruthfully fabled to kill every living thing within miles). Though a natural loner myself, and with the unfair advantage of hindsight, I at least would prefer to be "one" inclusively rather than exclusively. For us all, the possibility of spiritual advancement is bound up with identity: who, or what, is able to advance on this plane? What exactly do I mean when I say "I", when *I* am aware, when *I* walk alone; who is this green child, wistful for Spirit?

This question mark is the inevitable conclusion of a preliminary cycle. The question must remain unanswered by the mind, for it is as far as the mind can reach in the search for the wicket gate, the start of the path. Theories are of no further use. If your concern is for the whole earth – the macrocosm, your primary aim must be wholeness for the self – the microcosm. Wholeness begets wholeness, and fragmentation begets fragmentation. Only a whole person can hope to *do* anything on a cosmic scale, or on a spiritual scale. All so far has been a summary before the event, a recollection of all available possibilities before even approaching that white gate which may be found along the path which leads out of the forest of the mind.

2: IN SEARCH OF WHOLENESS

Soul Contents Include Bad as well as Good

I have already mentioned that one's less acceptable psychic contents are as much a part of the soul as one's more angelic characteristics: indeed, one might say, the greater the soul's capacity the more likely is it to carry widely varied contents. Some people may be of the same quality through and through, but I doubt it. Most of us are thoroughly varied and are sure to include the bad along with the good – what people consider to be good often turns out to be bad, and what people *consider* to be their bad side they will usually prefer to keep hidden.

Sexual content is probably the first characteristic to be affected when purification of soul contents begins to take place (through the action of the spiritual movement of *Subud* to which I shall return later), and it is probably the last too. It is after all the means by which the Almighty delegates a small part of the continuous process of creation, and the means by which we all enter this life. Plainly, the sexual function *should* be unadulterated and direct, as nature intended, as a male-female transaction devoted exclusively to producing offspring. That is clearly "God's will". But equally clearly present-day humans are more complicated and sophisticated than this view allows, and many of us are bound to fall short of the ideal. But deviation from the sexual ideal is not the real issue where soul-contents are concerned in their relationship to the field of the Spirit. The real issue is the usually unsuspected influence of the natural forces all around us, existing as vibrations or instinctual impulses. Think of the influence of materiality, which encourages us to treat ourselves and others as though we or they were merely things – as sex objects perhaps. Think of the influence of plant sex – the apparently irresponsible scattering of pollen, the apparently indiscriminate rape that results. Think of the influence of animal sex, all those widely varying instincts of creatures ranging from the smallest insect to the largest whale, all concentrating on the urge to mate when their season arrives.

Accepting the Shadow

Carl Gustav Jung formulated the existence of the "shadow" as the darkest part of the personal unconscious mind, the part of the psyche which retains all the factors which have been rejected by the conscious mind as being too horrendous or unpleasant to contemplate. A few unusually religious people, monks and imams alike, tend to suppress their baser instincts in favour of what they consider to be "holiness", and these people are particularly prone to encounter problems with their own psychic shadow. This happens particularly if they are fortunate enough to find their souls "opened" by the presence of Spirit. When this spiritual opening occurs, some of their nastier traits are bound to come spilling out like goblins released from an underground cell, announcing their presence noisily and forcefully. As a rule, we would prefer our shadow to remain hidden.

> Black as a raven's wing
> and twice as evil
> this apparition lodges in my soul and claims the right
> to haunt and howl and lurk within
> a demon doubly cursed yet countenanced
> a tenant in the basement flat
> he will not go because I bid him stay
> my shadow, my soul mate
> I cherish him
> though I dare not look him in the face.

This can be an unexpected and unnerving cause of dismay. Even respected religious leading figures, finding their own shadow publicly exposed in this way, have felt obliged to abandon their search for God at the very gateway to the path. Denying ownership of their own souls, they may convince themselves that they have been tricked into the presence of Satan and his demons, rather than the holy Spirit. They will then very likely find themselves fallen uncomfortably between two stools. As their souls will have been at least partially opened, they can never again return to their comfortable former state with sincerity. Through pride, they will have denied themselves access to the true path.

The point is this: never allow yourself to be dismayed into denying your own contents, at least to yourself. On the everyday level of heart and mind, you will have to let these contents emerge in order for them to be dispersed on the spiritual level. As they are part of your soul, they will be spoken of when the opened soul speaks, and acted out when the opened soul moves, and the basest characteristics tend to be disturbed first. My comments are intended to pre-empt the process and help it along by removing the sting. It is always best to avoid attention from psychiatrists (or witchdoctors according to your cultural background), not because they would be incapable of uncovering such things, but because they cannot really remove them. They may even reinforce them by making them seem acceptable, or even desirable. Faults at this deep level are not merely cases of mistaken thinking or disturbed emotions; they are part and parcel of the soul and, as such, are beyond the reach or capabilities of human therapy. The therapy needed at this level can operate only in the realm of spirit.

Ordinary suppressed memories as well as the more deeply repressed ones, of course, form a major part of Jung's shadow. Discovering this aspect of oneself is not by any means a "*Subud* process", but it is something that can be done at any time by a simple process of self-analysis: by the technique of sitting quietly, and allowing the relaxed mind to drift back in time, noting the points in one's life at which one seemed to have experienced a change of attitude, a change of feelings towards oneself or others. Once these points have been identified, one should be able to understand the reason for those changes, the factors that brought them about. There may well be a common theme, or a thread linking them all. What, in your everyday life, existed before, that did not apparently exist afterwards? It must have gone somewhere; and whatever those characteristics are or were, their substance is the very substance of one's personal shadow.

Astrology and the Threefold Cycle

This sort of thing is decidedly *Anwas* and pre-*Subud*, but for me it provided the first inkling of "soul" as a driving source of energy which should be allowed to lead. In my case it was intended as a session of self-analysis to counter an attack of depression at the age of twenty eight, and it certainly worked for me. A little later when I started taking an interest in astrology (as many people do when they are "searching"), I discovered that it corresponded exactly with the cyclical "rebirth" known to serious astrologers. This is an occasion that involves casting off preconceptions and inherited attitudes, and switching over to soul leadership, that is, allowing your own innermost self to guide rather than depending on one's old ideas of how things should be. A second natural opportunity occurs in everybody's life seven years later, at the age of thirty five – the discovery of an astrological "new-found identity".

If you say "that's nonsense!" you are probably still within the first cycle, and have these exciting incidents still to come. For me the experience came as a profound feeling of relief, the lifting of a great weight from my shoulders. I am not implying that a breakthrough can occur only at these ages, but it seems likely that all factors at those times militate towards its successful completion. In fact, the experience corresponds very neatly with the achievement of *satori* by many a Buddhist monk in the past. The sheer contrast of being able to "let go" after the stress of struggling with an apparently insuperable problem – the problem in Zen of trying to grasp one's own mind – produces a sense of euphoria and an intense emotional relief. In any case, a little self-observation will probably show that our lives are to a large extent governed by the twelve sections of the zodiac, proceeding by seven-year stages. Astrological tradition can prove remarkably useful when tracking the course of your own life, provided you accept Jung's conclusion regarding the value of astrology as an ancient system of psychology, and accept synchronicity as a legitimate phenomenon replacing the illogicality of astrological "influence". A poetic view is not out of place:

Aries

> Your coming to awareness: the act of being born,
> The inevitable weight of needs and fears
> Which you feel compelled to urgently project.
> Discovering how everything is done,
> Observing, learning from your peers
> And elders; to watch and to detect.
>> This, then, is your substitute for heaven,
>> Lasting till the age of seven.

Taurus

> An emotional discovery: your sensuality,
> Always looking inward at your feelings;
> Taking pleasure in the sense of your enjoyment,
> The while you treasure your security.
> There is a selfish streak in all your dealings,
> With personal considerations to augment.
>> You feel the need for family routine,
>> At least until you reach fourteen.

Gemini

> Fitting in, adapting to the world around you,
> Always looking outward with desire.
> Ever-changing, mobile, effervescent,
> Aspiring, striving, reaching ever higher.
> Relishing the moment to explain and argue
> −The ageless universal adolescent.
>> Sensing, tuning in to everyone,
>> Lasting till you're twenty-one.

Cancer

> Digging in, you search for self-protection
> Looking inward for a homely base.
> Though you seldom feel you find perfection,
> Your opinions have the gravity of facts.
> You look all psychic dangers in the face,
> Primed and ever ready to repel attacks.
>> 'Daring' is your psychic breastplate,
>> Till you reach the age of twenty-eight.

57

Leo

> Looking outwards at your world, you find conviction,
> The confidence to redefine yourself.
> You seldom feel the need for backing down.
> Some doubts are growing, causing inner friction;
> But with intuition bringing psychic health,
> You feel you truly wear the victor's crown!
>> Though there be doubts, you're totally 'alive',
>> And so you stay until you're thirty-five.

Virgo

> Those doubts have grown until they take command
> Compelling you to find another way.
> You criticise yourself until you find
> A firmer principle for life, your doubts allay,
> And give a firmer base on which to stand,
> A place where you may find true peace of mind:
>> A guidebook that will see you through
>> Until the time you're forty-two.

Libra

> Now comes a time to ruminate and ponder
> Your expressive needs. You yearn for harmony
> And greater unity with all mankind.
> And, forward looking, feel the need to wander,
> Continuing your life's great epic journey:
> Emotional, intellectual and physical combined.
>> You feel that everything must fall in line
>> Until you reach the age of forty-nine.

Scorpio

> Now inward-looking once again, intense,
> Casting new light on all that went before.
> For the first time now you feel you're seeing sense:
> Your previous hopes seem ineffectual,
> And yearning, penetrating to the very core,
> You seek solutions far more intellectual.
>> The time has come to penetrate to basics,
>> And so it bides until you're fifty-six.

58

Sagittarius

> You look out from your personal stronghold,
> Convinced that there is something there,
> Some major factor that you need to change,
> Something that you need to find, but where?
> The time has come, you feel, to play it bold,
> To let your talents much more widely range;
> > There has to be a goal: what can it be?
> > This doubt goes on until you're sixty-three.

Capricorn

> Quite suddenly it comes to your good sense
> Having beaten your poor head against the wall;
> You need to settle down to steady work again.
> With so much wonder in the world withal,
> Self-discipline will bring you independence,
> Especially if you think 'no pain, no gain'.
> > You need to work, and find the energy
> > To keep you busy till you're seventy.

Aquarius

> Looking out again and wondering what to do
> You think of novel ways to come to terms
> With life's great mystery, the need to live
> With what you gained before. Your mind affirms
> The unconventional approach, to give
> The world a taste of something new.
> > You strive until you think this has been given:
> > A period lasting till you're seventy-seven.

Pisces

> As you look inward, increasingly withdrawn
> Impressions strike you from within.
> The life you've lived has lent you hope,
> And faith, and reassurance, gained therein.
> You find the precious means by which to cope,
> And await the coming of a spiritual dawn.
> > As death's dark angel shuts the final door,
> > The total lifespan of the sage is eighty-four.

The deep psychological contents of the soul are not entirely arbitrary, nor are they entirely the result of childhood experiences and so on. They are built-in as part of nature's plan – or as part at least of what mankind has become with respect to nature's plan. In astrology, the age of eighty four years is sometimes called "the lifespan of the patriarch", and it comprises three twenty eight year laps of the circuit, three cycles of the astrological "houses", three transits through all the psychological possibilities available for an individual. These three twenty eight year phases are known respectively as the cycle of the body, the cycle of the soul, and the cycle of Spirit. One's "point of self" travelling through these cycles passes in turn through four seven year phases: the intuitional, the emotional, the physical and the intellectual phases. Older people can usually identify the various stages in their own lives without much difficulty. One can certainly recognise and recall the frustrations, the reappraisals, and the new realisations that have corresponded in one's own life with these "mundane" astrological stages.

The first cycle is concerned chiefly with one's vessel for life on earth. During childhood and young adulthood, a person's physical needs are of prime importance, and his ethical guide will be the influence of his family and the cultural rules of his community and race – the moral and religious restraints that he has inherited. Having lasted for twenty eight years this cycle, on its completion, represents a fulfilment of all that is past. The whole cycle of human life with all its available possibilities, for that individual, has been completed in just twenty eight years, but on a personal and ancestral level only. Then it must start again on a more exalted level.

The second passage through the twelve astrological houses is called the soul cycle, not because it applies more particularly to the inner self than did the preceding cycle, but because a person's soul comprises his or her whole contents, and not merely the inherited parts. This time the characteristics stirred within and rising to the surface are of a deeper nature. The time for cultural tradition should be past when a person reaches the age of twenty eight. The soul is now the leader, and rebirth into the first house of the second cycle should herald the awakening of inner awareness. Rather than a ready-made set of moral restraints and beliefs, a person's guide now should be his or her entire psychic content, both good and bad.

The third and final revolution of this great spiral is the cycle of Spirit, reached when a person has passed the age of fifty six. Speaking still in astrological terms, it is time now for influences from beyond materiality to infiltrate the smothering layers symbolised by the zodiac. As the product and culmination of the two previous cycles, the "mundane houses" of the self this time are occupied with an eye to the future. A person's guidance now should come, via the soul, from beyond both himself and his ancestors. The older person's ethical guide may be called the "collective experience", the spiritual principle, or even the Holy Spirit, depending upon his or her individual destiny and beliefs.

New-found Freedom

To return to the point of completion of the first and the start of the second cycle at the age of twenty eight, this "new-found freedom" will be felt as an unexpected boost – a major step forward – when a person has been actively searching for his or her own soul. Anyone who passes through this stage successfully will, by means of a suddenly acquired intuitive driving force, have regained contact with that forgotten soul, lost since babyhood. They will seem to have gained a new instinctive knowledge of their own capabilities, a new boost in confidence. However, lacking Spirit, they are unlikely to realise what has happened. But with this renewal there will probably arise a certain yearning for some kind of contact with spirituality. Old neuroses may seem to have disappeared, and to the mind which has become painfully aware of its own limitations, a fresh intuitive grasp of the situation will coincide with a refreshing sense of freedom from stifling conventional restraints.

Cyclic rebirth through the mundane houses is always a time of great significance. If one's inspiration is not accepted and followed, if one is unwilling to face the ordeal of impending rebirth the psyche may choose to remain within the symbolic womb of becoming, and languish on the level of ancestral culture. We all know individuals (and sometimes whole nations) to whom this seems to have happened. But if all goes well according to the cosmic plan, symbolic rebirth means that the individual becomes free to abandon total dependence on his inherited, ancestral past, and (whilst retaining inherited wisdom as necessary), to concentrate on building a new future based solidly on the individual personality, his or her own soul-contents in their entirety.

A Return to "Instinct"

A person in his or her late twenties, then, should be living by intuition, "following his instincts". He will be aware of his own capabilities as never before, and this artless and quite unconscious faculty can give him the urge to look more deeply within his own being. Through becoming aware of a mysterious capacity that he did not previously possess, he may well catch a glimpse of new and still more mysterious worlds open to exploration. Of course, the flash of intuition that helped to realign his progress was not the result of his own cleverness. It was merely an automatic and perfectly natural function of his own inner nature; a straight-forward cyclic rebirth into the first mundane house. It is only as he approaches the close of his second intuitional phase, towards the age of thirty five, that he will begin to have doubts about the wisdom of continuing his intuitive or instinctive course, correct though he knows that course to have been. Now that his intuitional capacity has developed to its fullest extent, it is the turn of the feelings to be dissatisfied. He realises that he must seek a new way of expressing himself, a new emotional creativity; a new identity. Perhaps the uninhibited exuberance of instinctive behaviour needs to be restrained, for his own good.

Whether seen in the context of a personal search for the true path, or merely as an interesting discovery through the study of astrology, or even as a stage in the psychological process which Jung called "individuation", all this is the reality of the personal soul – the "lower soul" – taking over the guiding role from the old moral, cultural and parental control. The famous analytical psychologist Carl Gustav Jung, whether he knew it or not, represented the very pinnacle of psychological possibilities within the spiritual sphere, and he was very familiar with this basic change that can take place. The changeover normally brings a profound sense of relief, and at least a noticeable degree of psychological freedom; but no particular "spiritual" element is involved, even during the second rebirth into the collective or Spirit cycle. In Zen, the adept's experiences following *satori* are said to be "nothing special"; the state is as natural and unexciting as fresh air is to breath, or pure water to a fish, and this is how it should be.

The process is one of uncovering rather than acquiring or creating anew. One may have practised self-analysis to help the transition along, but that is as far as *Anwas* practices should go; any further work on the self at this stage is, in my experience, particularly undesirable. The apprehension of "soul" may bring with it strange new perceptions – a flooding to awareness of contents which were previously unconscious; but, however wonderful, these perceptions belong to the realm of psychology and the occult and not to the spiritual field. Additional work on the idea of "self" can only create an *Anwas* shield of subtle mind-body, cutting off the soul from the wholeness which always surrounds it, and which should be allowed to fill it.

A Plethora of Systems and Techniques

Nowadays there seem to be hundreds of systems or techniques and numerous self-help books aimed at improving the brain, improving the understanding, creating some kind of soul awareness, creating something "real" within, finding ways to command the life forces

63

of materiality. In my opinion these methods should be treated with caution. Strength of mind may be an admirable (or at least much admired) quality when directed towards the sensory non-spiritual world – towards the everyday, material world of commerce and enterprise, entertainment and education. But strength of mind coupled with spiritual aims tends to breed spiritual fanaticism, which, I think, is fanaticism of the very worst kind.

Whether it be aimed inwards towards the self, or equally "outwards" towards God, the most likely outcome of dedicated concentration of the mind in this context is the inadvertent creation of an "artificial soul", a subtle mental-emotional vehicle that will surround the true self and carry it suspended, as it were, in a state of limbo. This, at any rate, is how it seems to me. The nature of one's beliefs will then be irrelevant, for they will be limited to the "self". Far from acting as a magnet to draw the influences of forces higher than the human (for which any sane person must long), a self-created "soul" can only act as a barrier against such influences, whether these are visualised as originating beyond or within the individual self.

The Personal and the Collective Unconscious

In psychological terms the initial breakthrough, the first rebirth within the threefold cycle, or the realisation of "soul", is the coming to awareness of the "personal unconscious". The second major breakthrough, the second rebirth, should be the coming to awareness of the "collective unconscious". It may be that you personally are content at this stage to let matters rest on a psychological footing, although I can assure you that they are not the same: there is a "great gulf fixed" between the psychological and the spiritual. Now, however, prior to receiving contact with Spirit, one's concern may well be directed towards the "true self", with the rich symbolism to be found within the collective unconscious being seen as a source of inspiration, and a spur to further progress.

It is the wilful brother, *Sahid Anwas*, who remains devoted to psychology to the unwitting exclusion of true spirituality. The philosophy of life favoured by *Sahid Anwar*, arrived at unconsciously from a less personal source, includes the understanding that true spirituality is to be found only within harmonious collectivity. It leads to the inevitable realisation that, in the end, "all are one". Yet despite the differences between East and West, between *Anwas* and *Anwar*, between the exclusively personal and the collective, standard western spiritual thought is not really unsympathetic towards the Buddhist view of self as the Supreme Being. As I have argued before, it is not a "selfish" view, self has ultimately to be greater than the collective unconscious, because it can contain it. As Jung explained: "Self is not only the centre, but also the circumference that encloses consciousness and the unconscious; it is the centre of this totality, as the ego is the centre of consciousness."

The Collective Self

The "collective self" is not something that can be constructed artificially. It is not the same thing as a gathering of like-minded seekers working together. Indeed, in my personal experience, communal efforts such as discussion groups or workshops, with this sort of aim in mind, almost invariably hinder rather than help individual progress towards understanding and change. The idea of "confusion" as defined by modern western standards seems more readily to fit a collaborative state rather than any attitude of the individual towards "inner truth" or, indeed, towards the "outer truths" of politics or race relations. I believe psychologists have often noticed that a body of people acting as a group tend to make less intelligent decisions and come to less sensible conclusions than would any of its individual members acting alone. It is as if they are drawing upon some primitive collective archetype at the expense of their sophisticated individual qualities. To paraphrase Jung's well-known remark: "A hundred intelligent heads gathered together add up to one monstrous hydrocephalus." But this phenomenon at least, with its seemingly individual over-ruling of acquired intellectual characteristics, does represent an unconscious movement, however slight, towards the inner self. It drops the first hint that this sphere of the inner self, paradoxical though it may seem, surrounds the outer personality, and even embraces the whole of the collective unconscious.

The Zen Search for Spontaneity

In analytical psychology the collective unconscious is said to be the source of human instinctive actions – an impulse to action without conscious motivation; the largely unknown background material acquired not only over the individual lifetime, but the combined experiences of the human race, the common field from which our individual consciousness emerges. Is this not the very impulse which produces *dhyana*, the human instinct? In Zen the tradition of the *koan* prompts the answering of considered questions with instantaneous and unconsidered observations, intended as a "direct pointing" to *dhyana*. Is not the source of the truly unconsidered answer also the collective unconscious? Neither analytical psychologists nor Zen masters have any way of knowing that spiritual spontaneity is already in the possession of certain people who value the power of submission to impersonal Spirit. The exercise of spiritual spontaneity, as those few fortunate people have discovered, cannot be achieved by looking to a personal Buddha-figure within. There is more to it than that.

All this seems to suggest that Zen is a useful pivot but a poor pilot. In its philosophical, if not its practical aspects, it seems acutely aware of its *Anwas* roots and the need to draw closer to *Anwar*. Zen has described its own process of thinking as "no-thought", and its own mind as "no-mind". This clearly acknowledges a deep feeling of need for true spontaneity – its need for the "happening" of unconsidered rather than premeditated action, whether the quality of that action is active or passive, controlled or relaxed. Seen from the outside, the Zen establishment seems to me to be searching and longing for some sort of truly instinctive spontaneity as a permanent state. This is, of course, the whole essence of the spiritual search: the discovery or at least the apprehension of that independent "inner guide" who will lead where destiny requires.

Analysis Precludes Wholeness

"Direct pointing" to *dhyana* by conjuring up odd fragmented snatches of spontaneity, hoping to illuminate a far greater self which remains to be discovered: it is rather like exploring a new landscape at dead of night in a thunderstorm, to be glimpsed only during those brief flashes of lightning. It brings to mind the astrological explanation of cyclic wholeness: apprehension of the "self" requires wholeness of perception, and is not an "intelligent" process. Intellect and wholeness tend to be incompatible, because the function of intellect is to break down wholes into recognisable parts by the process of analysing them. The moment analysis commences, the possibility of perceiving wholeness recedes.

The emotional function of feeling is no more successful than intellect as a tool with which to understand the soul, because soul must necessarily include the whole being within itself – and this is no more than personal wholeness. When that personal wholeness becomes transformed into universal wholeness – when soul "becomes" Spirit – intellect, thoughts, feelings, heart and mind, can play no part other than that of mute observer. When it occurs, it is an unmistakeable and very strange experience, and analysis has no part to play in it. The moment appraisal asserts itself, when the mind starts to analyse and the heart starts to feel the quality of any identifiable part of the experience, wholeness is automatically sacrificed, and with it all possibility for that moment, of apprehending the spiritual self.

It is as if the true self – a seed of the whole inner self – occupies a gap between thought and action, obscured by feeling. What seems to thinking, reasoning man to be a senseless void, an absence of awareness, is in fact the realm of the *dharma* of which *dhyana* is but a pale reflection: the seat of the true human instinct,

67

the *Aras Allah* of the Sufi. To realise the *dharma* fully is to realise one's own Buddha nature. For *Sahid Anwar* the submissive acceptance of this silent void, once the seed has been sown, is to allow an inflowing of Holy Spirit, to raise the lowly status of "soul" by accepting Spirit as guide. This is the beginning of the "true path". No-one can say with certainty that *Sahid Anwas* cannot achieve the same ends; real results are equally real however attained. But certainly they are easier to attain by not striving, by not taking thought, by merely "getting on" with whatever you have to do.

A 15th century Zen anthology of poems, songs and sayings applicable to the *koan*, has it

Sitting in silence, without action,
Spring arrives and the new grass grows by itself.

Natural growth and real progress by both nature and art are best accomplished without the purposeful intervention of coarse thought and deliberate physical action, simply because, to be meaningful, to have spiritual content, they have to arrive via the inner, on an instinctual level.

The aim of Zen may traditionally remain unexpressed by its exponents ("Those who know, do not speak; those who speak, do not know"), and many millions of words must have been spoken and written to substantiate this. But if it works as it should, it can never go beyond the discovery of the personal lower soul. After that, there is nothing to be done but to follow this new-found guide. When the soul comes to life, a path makes itself known to the individual seeker. The direction and quality of this path is a matter of fate, and its ultimate destination a matter of destiny. This is the "soul" that has as its spiritual centre of gravity the various mysterious life forces of nature: the instinctual forces of the material level; the network of instincts on the plant level; the instincts and desires of the animal level; the guided movements of the instinctual human level of being, and a truly evergreen place.

Every school of spiritual thought, every religion, every language even, has its own definitions of the principle of soul, and the terms with which to express it. This is the lower human soul, which may not differentiate between mental, emotional or moral extremes, which through good and bad alike knows only its own contents – contents that will include all lifetime experiences and inheritances, past and present, high and low.

The Need for Symbols to Express Reality

Officially, Zen knows nothing of soul or Spirit, and already I approach the point where instinct must be allowed to take over from anxious mind, and Zen must be left behind to find its own way out of its self-sown forest. But I shall continue to use its arguments and its symbolism to mark the way, for there are no arguments or symbolism to use in the field of Spirit, in spiritual reality. Zen rightly insists that "self" is indeed a symbol, an idea, not to be confused with reality. We unavoidably form an idea of ourselves outside of ourselves, such is the power of mind to construct symbols when facts are difficult to grasp. It seems an essential adjunct of human personality. It is only when the abstract symbol is taken for material reality that errors and confusion arise, as with the dog that shakes imaginary rain from its coat whenever it hears the thunder. As, indeed, when religious devotees confuse the symbols of their religion with spiritual reality.

The nature of "self" is again the crux of the problem. The Zen ethic of scorning the egoistic symbol of "self" – a symbol that both westerners and easterners habitually hold dear – is also the Gurdjieff ethic, and both, it seems to me, are equally transitional phases in man's development. When Gurdjieff spoke of "remembering oneself" he meant being aware of the non-egoistic self, the true "I" behind the myriad moods. At that very moment when one turns comfortably to one's own established attitudes, to one's own unthinking acceptance of one's "self", his pupils were to pull themselves up short, to recall their real, non abstracted, non identified, non symbolic self.

Accepting "Self" as All-Inclusive

Jung's "self" more specifically includes all its own characteristics, both the "conscious" and the "unconscious" within itself, and stands in opposition to ego, which always tends to reject what it considers to be the inferior or undesirable elements of itself. The personal unconscious mind of the self is indeed difficult to accept in its entirety, for the simple reason that it remains "unconscious". The condition Jung called "individuation" involved, or involves, the coming to awareness of these unconscious characteristics, which are normally the least acceptable features of oneself. Attaining "self" in Jungian terms thus involves the complete acceptance of all that may be unwanted and irrational in one's nature, as well as the more desirable features.

The foundation of all Zen riddles in their search for spontaneity is already self, in the broadest sense, acknowledging it as the all-embracing Tao. The original aim of yoga, and particularly of Chinese yoga, was the eventual development of an immortal spirit-body which would depend on an equal interplay of *Yang* and *Yin*, forces high and low, light and dark, masculine and feminine. This in turn, of course depends on the bringing to light of the dark contents of the personal unconscious mind – the process of Jung's principle of individuation. Zen inherited the concept of self as the supreme principle, the ultimate oneness of being.

The Limitations of Yoga

Many people take up yoga as the next step along the path. Indian yoga in particular is a classic example of *Anwas* practice. In its more physical forms – especially *hatha* yoga as commonly adopted by westerners – it brings undoubted benefits in terms of glowing health, self confidence, mental and physical relaxation and a feeling of well-being. Certainly I can vouch for the fact that *hatha* yoga really works, and these beneficial results are often taken as evidence that yoga is a "good" practice, or one at least which helps to carry the inner self in the right direction. But however beneficial they may be on the surface, in the outer layers of mind and body, the results of yoga practice are still confined within the bounds of materiality: that is to say, within the realm of "passion". Yoga will certainly fill the lower soul with yogic results, but this soul is filled with everything else as well, and such results will leave Spirit and *Jiwa* untouched, unmoved, and unheard.

Having said that, I may add too that yoga is an *unnecessary* participant in the search for spiritual reality. Do not forget that yoga is only the "Third Way" of work on the mind. Its intensive practice over long periods brings an enviable serenity to its devotee, whose untroubled mind is well symbolised by the lotus flower that floats on a calm lake. But it is the lake itself, and not the flower, that is the karmic reservoir of the inner self. It is not merely a case of allowing the silt of the mind to settle; the sublimation of thought, you might say, produces oil which rises to the surface in a thinly diffused layer, so that at first glance all seems peaceful. There are no waves, but only the restfully changing colours of the oil moving gently across the water. But fierce creatures may lurk unsuspectedly in the depths, and a stick thrust through the surface could stir them into a state of fury. Primordial demon-ridden slime may lie fathoms thick on the bottom of the lake, and though the process will inevitably shatter the effect of calm and disrupt the lotus flower, the whole vessel really needs draining and dredging if the yogi is to escape the karmic consequences of his own unsuspected contents. As the symbol well portrays, the base of yoga is materiality, and its surface is the base of the spiritual plant force – the world of plants at its most passive, the "clever vegetable" resting on the lowest spiritual force, the satanic *roh*. The real barrier, the gateway to the path, has still not been opened.

> The lotus seat,
> the body rigid, locked
> unmoveable, unmoved by all that stirs,
> forcing the mind to concentrate upon itself.

Thoughts and emotions overruled
mind set, unmoveable, unmoved
soul locked beneath the armour plate:
no ill can enter here!
No evil influence can assail the yogi
dedicated to his cause.

The lotus flower
that floats serenely beautiful,
upon the water of the self
unruffled, undisturbed,
that perfect flower draws sustenance
deep fathoms down
from layers of putrefaction.

Early eastern yogis, being relatively free from all the distractions that surround modern people, may well have been comparatively pure inwardly, and to that extent free of karmic content. In today's world, East as well as West, clamorous influences flood in from all sides. Actions and attitudes inspired by habitual use of the coarse passions – or perhaps, their use of us – create contents which accumulate continuously, and the more deeply entrenched of these contents are handed down to successive generations through the karmic as well as the genetic line of inheritance.

The Will of the Yogi Creating an Obstacle

All this serves to anchor the human soul more firmly to the earth. The lotus of the yogi mind retains the appearance of serenity only through its own strength of will, and the lake of the soul remains tranquil only whilst this mind lives and retains its habitual power of concentration. And if or when the accomplished yogi finally feels a need to change and follow the way of *Sahid Anwar,* it is the hard-won *kundalini* of his creative imagination, once valued, that will now make it difficult for him to receive the gift of Spirit with sincerity. Having trained his mind to resist outside influences, he will tend to reject the vibration of so fine an influence originating beyond his own centre of gravity. The knack of concentrating the mind and quietening the emotions and the body, so painfully acquired through a prolonged effort of will, ironically turns out to be the very thing that makes spiritual receiving difficult when the chance to do so arises. The possibility of attaining the reality of Susila Budhi Dharma will have been made that much more remote by this yogic process of veneering over the inner self. This is the unsuspected fruit, in this present age, of the "Third Way" of the yogi. One may perhaps contrast this with the emotion-based "Second Way" of the monk, for whom it will be the rejection of what may be seen as heretically unfamiliar ideas, rather than the voluntarily acquired *kundalini* that will be likely to preclude any further receiving.

The symbolic, imaginary "self" to which things happen, may be questioned as a concept equally critically from the viewpoints both of "will" and of "submission"; both from Zen and from beyond Zen. The feeling that "self" possesses mind is a purely subjective one. In Zen, both subject and object are seen as one, uniting the experience with the one who experiences, the knower with that which is known. Materiality still controls the conscious self. The *hatha* yogi, whilst controlling his breath, may consider: "I breathe", but he might just as well consider: "it breathes me". Unwittingly, in using his will, he is submitting to the power of materiality. As Pak Subuh was wont to ask his followers when he perceived that they were attracting the constricting power of material will at the moment when they should have been feeling the penetrating release of divine submission: "Are you sitting on the chair ... or is the chair sitting on you?" – were they still unwittingly being used by the life forces of materiality?

Danger of Creating a False Soul

All this boils down to the fact that to "try" to do anything on the spiritual plane is to try to move mountains with the bare hands – to manipulate something that is far larger than the "self" and far stronger than the original spontaneous mind. It is only the advantage of hindsight than enables me to see the dangers inherent in using *Anwas* methods to rediscover the personal soul or *sukma*. Such efforts can miss their aim and lead instead to the creation of an extra, unsuspected, parasitical "soul", as an unwanted brand of "oneness".

To hark back to Gurdjieff and his intent to create "deputy steward" in order to counter the multiplicity of "I's", we have seen that any such attempt may well succeed. But if this newly created deputy steward is mistaken for "steward", or even more deeply mistaken for the master of the house himself, the result will be a crystallisation of spontaneity, a subtle mind-body that acts as a hard shell to cover the soul, to conceal rather than reveal the true Buddha-self, and which may even preclude the intervention of Spirit. In setting out to discover his own faculties of intelligent, critical appraisal, experience suggests that *Sahid Anwar*, that people of faith, must needs submit to the collective experience. "Self", though personal, must embrace the apparently far greater collective self in order to come fully to awareness. *Collective* oneness becomes the focus of one's aim; the brotherhood of man; the realisation of "All one body, we!" It is precisely this compassionate spiritual collectivity – and it doesn't matter that one's personal concept of this collectivity may be the collective unconscious, or the Holy Spirit, or even Almighty God – that can enter the individual. The self, the soul, can encompass it and, by being assimilated, it can assimilate the personal soul into itself. This is truly the beginning of the path to the source, a step towards Universal Being.

It is so easy to become proud or self important. Self in this sense has never greatly concerned *Sahid Anwar;* humility is far safer ground on which to stand. Trying to identify the true self is characteristic and often the particular weakness of *Sahid Anwas.* So many dangers are inherent in any disciplined method of seeking, whether the discipline comes from without or within. It is easy when pursuing Spirit to become lost in the forest of the mind. The 9th century "Essentials of the Doctrine of Mind" pointed out:

By their very seeking for the Buddha nature, they lose it; by using the Buddha to seek the Buddha, by using the mind to grasp mind ... they will create a mind over and above mind, seek the Buddha outside themselves, and remain attached to forms, practices, and performances − all of which is harmful, and not the way to attain supreme knowledge.

The Distinction between Heart and Mind

As the seat of emotion, the heart is often the driving force behind religious conviction. The mind, the rational intellect, is often behind the urge to seek the true self. When the two come together the combined effect, often enough, can be to create a fanatical hardening of purpose. Sometimes, as in Christianity, they may work in opposition to produce that "glorious strife" which, so says the hymn, may win the crown of life. Buddhism, and in particular Zen Buddhism, because of its roots and the cultural background of the majority of its practitioners, and because of its abhorrence of the "split mind", makes no allowance for the distinction between mind and heart. Where thoughts and emotions are perceived to have separate directions, as they often are in western thought, the advantages can be great. Certainly the idea itself is divisive, but every creation is the "third" of a triad. A certain degree of fragmentation is the first step towards unity. There is a corresponding freedom of spiritual perception. The heart can stand aside, perhaps to the left, and the mind can move across, perhaps to the right, to expose an opening in the passions, the better to observe and evaluate the blank screen of the basic soul. In this way the concealing curtains can be made to move apart, leaving the self to wait in patient anticipation for the spiritual show to begin.

I speak from personal experience when I say that, as witnesses to spiritual phenomena, neither heart nor mind can take part in their own experiences. Mind of itself must not be moved during the process, for consciously either to direct thought or to stop thought is to take thought. Even in denying analysis or the desire to analyse, the mind is already analysing, choosing, weighing and balancing – even perhaps playing the role of Spirit, whilst the heart is often all too eager to play the balancing role of soul. It is not always easy to separate thoughts from emotions. Only when the two are identified and perceived as distinct, can they separate easily and understand their own limitations.

Certainly, not everyone is familiar with the concept of heart and mind as representing two distinct functions of the human condition. Though it has always been an integral part of the Judaic and Christian traditions, in present-day Islam the distinction seems to have become lost, or dismissed as irrelevant. Even when the duality is acknowledged, the act of bringing together thoughts and feelings can seem to the egoistic self a wholly integrating process, creating a oneness of purpose and a sense of worth. But impartial observation suggests that to combine these two, the cold thoughts and the hot emotions, is to become lukewarm – to start a movement towards the encapsulation or isolation of the soul. This certainly seems to be the inference in the *Revelation of St John the Divine*. When the distinction between heart and mind is neither made nor felt, the fact lends strength to the arrogant assumption that "we are gods". But when the division between these two functions is perceived and accepted to the extent of being taken for granted, it can open the way to seeing exactly how lowly our collective and individual spiritual state has become:

These things saith the Amen, the faithful and true witness, the beginning of the creation of God; I know thy works, that thou art neither cold nor hot: I would thou wert cold or hot. So then because thou art lukewarm, and neither cold nor hot, I will spue thee out of my mouth. Because thou sayest, I am rich, and increased with goods, and have need of nothing; and knowest not that thou are wretched, and miserable, and poor, and blind, and naked.

Cultural and Racial Preconceptions

Worldwide attitudes towards "soul" as an independent entity are bound to vary. Certain racial groups sometimes seem almost committed to bringing about encapsulation or closing off of the soul. Some peoples seem more open than others in their attitude towards spiritual influence. To some western races who are in the habit of observing the foibles of others, a lack of distinction between heart and mind may seem to explain the old chestnut of "eastern inscrutability". Members of some races seem normally to possess a deep inner calm, but, often when least expected, they prove liable to erupt into impassioned action. When human communication is based on the passions, groups with differing passions are liable to find themselves speaking a different language at all levels of meaning.

No pejorative implication is intended in describing racial characteristics in these terms, because we can draw a powerful parallel between the races of the earth and the differing passions of the individual human soul. Each different racial type has a clear counterpart within the innermost being of each one of us. It has to be so, and in this we can envisage the emergence of a true "brotherhood of man". Any correlation between the colours of mankind and their inner natures should be seen as wholly symbolic, because racial differences are those of passion, and not of spirituality. The principle may perhaps best be expressed in humorous terms and, even more so, in poetic vein: we are all unique as individuals, and yet each one of us embodies the whole human race at the level of passions, at the level of soul:

A black man, red man, yellow man, white man –
Forget the racist theme.
They are one race: they are all brothers
in a dream.
And in this dream the brothers live together
in the soul
of everyone whoever lived, since humans first began.

I think of it this way because I am a male,
but you may call them sisters too, for what it's worth.
Our wish, our indignation, our desire:
our coloured passions give us energy
but hold us down to earth.
They are the elements, the bloods, the fire,
the soul concealed beneath the veil.

You may even see yourself,
in this strange fleeting fashion
when you are in a quiet frame of mind,
as black, or red, or yellow, or white,
for this reflects your passion,
and the driving force that you are sure to find
when anger, envy, greed or lust reveals itself!

But recall the holy spirit which descended like a dove
upon one wholly balanced soul.
Atoned – at one – the balanced soul is brown,
for black and red and yellow and white
combined can wear the crown,
and the family of man in peace can all unite:
For the brown soul, in this scheme of things, is love!

Characteristics Corresponding to Inner Passions

Certain races tend to be more permeable than others, more
penetrable by higher influences, and this largely depends upon the
way they think of themselves. One particular branch of mankind
tend to see themselves in material terms, and no doubt because of
this peculiar trait have historically been treated unsympathetically
by other races, moved around and used as if they were indeed
material objects. Such people sometimes seem to be standing too
close to their own situation to see it in true perspective. In the
emotional and religious sense they may see themselves as
belonging to, as being "one with" the earth; but, lacking a more
broadly based viewpoint, they tend to miss out on the fruits of the
earth. In looking to the earth for wholeness, but lacking the knack
of observing materiality in a practical way, in the instinctive

process of acquisition they tend to see only the immediate value of other life forms sharing that earth. Misplaced enthusiasm leads to unbalanced development, and they usually find themselves denied the good things of life and, quite often literally, living in the desert.

Another distinct branch of mankind have also found themselves to be at a considerable disadvantage. Tied to the earth as though rooted in the soil, they have always felt themselves to be "one with nature". Their religious emotions prompt them to look downwards to the earth, where they see the subtle nature of other life forms that share it, and are able to experience the *dharma* – the God-given nature – of these wild creatures. But, limited to one kind of living and one kind of environment, they tend to be quite unadaptable. These are plant people at root. Tiny seedlings may transplant well, but in the case of mature plants, the process of uprooting and transplanting is rarely successful. When places and conditions change, whole communities or even nations tend to disappear. Through this brand of specialisation at the expense perhaps of the complementary passions of tenacity, fecundity, pragmatism and adaptability, some of them have all but extinguished their own spark of life.

There is another and much larger branch of mankind who are not tied to earth in this way. Lacking the unquestioned security a feeling of "oneness" with nature brings, they frequently feel obliged to compensate by seeking ways to attract divine guidance, good fortune and "luck" to themselves. Like the animals, they are quick to defend the boundaries of their territories, although they are free to roam and adaptable to changing circumstances. But as humans following their religious instincts they are still in the habit of looking downwards to the earth and to their own ancestors with reverence, as though attempting through conformity to rediscover the security of ancient roots.

Another branch of mankind tends to look to the future, seldom taking the earth or the past too seriously. People such as this have the distinction of self-reliance. More individualistic and

79

perhaps less sociable than some other races, they are the observers and analysers of the world, and when they look inward they are the most likely to "see" the fragmentation that exists within themselves and others. Chiefly they value strength of mind and the power of logic, but they recognise emotional warmth as a distinct function. They tend to see other races as more "spiritual" than themselves, though the opposite is quite often the case. When seeking spiritual integration they tend to look for something extra outside of themselves, and beyond the earth, so in this they tend towards the principle of *Anwar.*

Still another large branch of humankind traditionally see themselves as being close to the spiritual, but through their long association with the principle of *Sahid Anwas* they tend to squander their opportunities, and their birthright, on questionable hierarchies and complicated ritual. It is natural for this racial group to assume spiritual and moral superiority over the rest of the world, mistaking the ancient inbuilt symbol for the reality. But whilst they look inside themselves for spiritual reality, they still feel it reasonable to seek a guru, both to give advice and to act as a catalyst that will bring about a spiritual reaction. For this reason their cultures tend to respect "holy men", and may look benignly on individuals who drop out of society as part of the search for personal enlightenment.

Seeking a Catalyst to Start the Reaction

Some individuals are prouder than others, but over and above these personal traits every race has its own distinctive brand of pride. Amongst European races, typically "every man is his own doctor of divinity", and the personal urge to seek a guru is largely absent. In so obscure a field as this, wherein knowledge is "unknowable" except through insight, nobody likes to feel outdone. Certainly neither in West nor East is there an intrinsic barrier between the individual and the "unknowable", between sleeping and waking, apart from the passions of everyday life that cloud the inner self. But in my experience something from beyond the self is certainly needed to help clear at least a narrow path through the restricting accumulation of passion – a catalyst that may start a self-sustaining reaction. In the end, whatever one's race, colour or creed, all must come to that final discovery: once a clear corridor has been perceived, once contact has been made, none can intervene; every soul stands at last before the power of the Absolute. The voice of the soul is always spontaneous, independent of thought, emotion, or physical action, but it needs the leaven in the lump, the spark of submissive divinity to bring it to life.

To cultivate spontaneity, working from the outside inwards, is a clear case of putting the cart before the horse. To *Sahid Anwar* both meditation and the "practice" of spontaneity are doomed attempts by his brother *Anwas* eventually to produce what *Anwar* already has without trying, the most elementary effects of his own submissive attitude. The hopelessness of "seeking" in this way comes to awareness following the realisation that what is being sought is already there; already here. To seek the Buddha nature, in the words of a 9th century Zen master, is like "riding the ox in search of the ox". So as an *Anwas* method of "not doing", Zen has to be direct – it can but point to truth in the expectation that budhi, that spiritual awakening, is already there, waiting to be realised. In this *Sahid Anwar* and *Sahid Anwas* are agreed: there is no real substitute for direct practical experience, and both symbols and theories are of little further use. By the beginning of the 1960s Pak Subuh Sumohadiwidjojo (and none knew better than he) was telling us that "the time for symbolism is past". Religions of course are wholly symbolic of spiritual reality, but by apparently rejecting symbolism in this way he was not suggesting that we abandon our traditional religions, however symbol-based they may be. The heart too needs satisfaction; needs, if only through the balm of the living symbol, to feel that it too is destined to be included in the scheme of things as an integral part of the ultimate whole. But he was pointing out that the time had already come when it was necessary to experience for oneself the reality of the inner life, the inner life of reality. The experience itself obviates the need for symbols and parables.

But of course symbols and parables are still necessary for the vast majority of people who have come to no understanding of the inner self, and certainly no experience of the ultimate reality. The case was similar when Jesus was preaching to the crowds, and his disciples, having experienced the reality for themselves, and knowing that parables are, almost by definition, wholly symbolic, questioned him thus (according to St Matthew's Gospel):

Why speakest thou unto them in parables? He answered and said unto them, Because it is given unto you to know the mysteries of the kingdom of heaven, but to them it is not given.

The spontaneous spiritual exercise of *Subud* actually is that experience, ongoing and self sustaining through conscious awareness. Through having been granted some degree of consciousness we are, or should soon be, able to recognise the heart as the impostor it loves to be when it pretends (or actually believes) that *it* is the "lord"; when it believes *itself* to be a god, or the soul, or Spirit, or a spirit guide, or the Buddha, or the Prophet Mohammed, or Jesus Christ; by being conscious enough to check the self-important mind, when it masquerades as *Aras Allah,* the seat of God.

The "Impossible Necessity" of Stopping Thoughts

Zen-inspired, the "instant understanding" of *satori* grasps the soul like a twining plant; it may be the choking grip of honeysuckle, or the sheltering embrace of ivy, but whether violent or gentle it has to acknowledge that basic reality, the source of all instinctual behaviour, remains spontaneous and cannot be understood or investigated by the mind. The twin tracks of *Anwas* and *Anwar* may still appear to run parallel. Whether or not the Zen aspirant tries to recapture the lost human instinct, seems irrelevant to its actual attainment. Clever brains can prove a stumbling block, because determination to relax the mind, to let go, far from achieving its aim can only strengthen the ego. (See how well I can relax my mind!) Relaxation with calm acceptance, that is the key. But to anyone with an active mind, it is easier said than done; it is not enough merely to think about not thinking. The impossibility of stopping thought with thought was summarised thus by a 17th century Japanese Zen master:

To use thought to stop thoughts is like trying to wash blood from a garment with blood. If the old blood be washed out, it is only to leave new blood in its place. The use of thought in this never-ending way is to cling to the wheel of birth and death. Thought is transient, so do not try to hold onto it, and do not try to reject it. Whether it is there or not, let it be. Thoughts are like images in a mirror. The cleaner the mirror, the clearer the reflection, but no image ever sticks to it. The Buddha mind is much clearer than a mirror, and infinitely more marvellous.

The appropriate attitude can arise spontaneously only when the everyday passions, hopes, fears and especially desires, are allowed to subside. This is the only way to the *Tao*, the ultimate path to reality. As a religious concept, the *Tao* was the historical precursor and ultimately the progenitor of Zen, via Hinduism and Buddhism. It may be surmised that Zen itself, in inheriting the virtues of Taoism, and in rejecting the self-clinging instincts of the Buddhists, originally had as its hoped-for aim the rediscovery of what was known in Taoist organisations as "virtuous movement", and in Zen as *miao-yung,* or "marvellous activity". It carried the meaning of the miraculous or magical quality of spontaneity – a wonderful involuntary spiritual exercise that is completely human in instinct, yet without human invention or intervention. Even then, this mystical phenomenon was little more than a faint folk memory. And only now, after a thousand years of baffled speculation, many of us have witnessed that it has finally returned to reality in the spontaneous and unwilled spiritual exercise of *Subud.*

Recapturing Miraculous Spontaneity

If I and others with a similar experience are to be believed, it can now truly be said that "spring arrives and the new grass grows by itself". To one who has stepped beyond Zen to receive and follow this wholly *Anwar* spiritual exercise – this spiritual exercise of *Subud* – all past efforts seem in retrospect only too plainly to have been aimed instinctively at recapturing this miraculous spontaneity. I say recapturing rather than capturing because, as the ancient Taoists doubtless knew, this spontaneous exercise is the original and perfectly natural instinctive movement of the inner self, guiding the body and the mind, a movement brought about through contact with Spirit, after having been lost at the original fall from grace – the expulsion from Eden. But how exactly is this essential contact with Spirit to be regained? As both the Upanishads and the New Testament stress, Spirit cannot be coerced. Man cannot choose Spirit; Spirit alone chooses.

All those years of striving, meditating, concentrating, were in vain. "Marvellous activity" could *never* have been introduced, as it were retrospectively, through the will. Once again we return to the age-old conflict between *Anwas* and *Anwar*, the great psychological division that was really behind the breaking away of Buddhism from its Hindu roots, and that we now know resulted in the development of Zen as a direct method of rediscovering original simplicity.

When Pak Subuh passed on his miraculous "contact", by so doing he instituted a far simpler and even more direct method of recapturing the essence of *Anwar*, and regaining Eden. Certainly, "the kingdom of heaven is within", and it is only from within that Spirit can manifest itself in man. But self is nothing without that indefinable Spirit, and though simple and direct, the path to be trod is narrow as a knife-edge. Any difficulties encountered are those already present within oneself. There is a great difference between the two similar-seeming acts: looking within oneself in the hope of *receiving* something of value; and looking within oneself with the intention of discovering and strengthening what is already there. One would perhaps think the former a more comfortable option, but frequently it proves the more difficult. The former opens the way to unlimited expansion and spiritual development; the latter, even whilst achieving its aims, tends to create a protective shell which can only preclude the possibility of further spiritual growth.

Seed of the Inner Self

We could say that the unmodified human soul is like the seed of a black acacia that needs to pass through fire before it can germinate – and the fire in this case is Spirit. Without this fire the tough outer coat of the seed – the self-made capsule – will not split. Inner growth in this case may result in a strengthening, not of the "spiritual" but of the occult. It may lead to very real magical powers and strange experiences; it may even lead to *nirvana*, the calm eye of the hurricane. But still through it all the germ, the soul, unable to experience wholeness, will remain forever trapped within the sphere of materiality – the awesomely powerful satanic force that is so much lower than the truly human state.

A truly humble attitude is needed in order to lay aside all preconceived ideas of self, and accept a power *greater* than the human. A submissive approach that, in the right circumstances, will leave the way open to a possible inflowing of spiritual impulses. To adopt such an approach is certainly a major step towards progressive freedom from the "power of Satan" and, later, from the power of the Green Man and the cycle of nature. Moreover, it is a freedom that does not require its participants to live in special circumstances either alone or in company, and it does not call for any of the ascetic practices so beloved of *Anwas* and his successors.

Recollections of an original "marvellous activity" exist everywhere as a folk memory, and not merely in Taoism or Zen. It comes to the fore in many forms of worship, as the placing together of the palms or lifting the arms in prayer. Whether instinctive or conditioned, it amounts to a collective recollection of a spontaneous physical movement derived from the unwilled spiritual movements of the soul. One can only speak from one's own experience. Christian worshippers of the charismatic persuasion and many others would claim the experience is already a familiar one, though in their case involvement by the heart and prompting by the mind inevitably impose a wholly misleading emotional burden and cast a shadow of doubt on what should be the untrammelled movement of the soul. Emotional movements are not at all the same thing, and the heart likes nothing better than to seek attention for itself.

A New-born Child Possesses Wisdom

It is fairly apparent that a very young child functions and moves by the promptings of human instinct, whatever term we wish to use to describe it. Long before the brain has developed ideas of its own, such a child can seem a fount of ancient wisdom, able to converse (without audible words) with any spiritually "ascending" adult whose inner state happens to correspond, and whose outer state is sensitive enough to be aware of it. For me, experiences such as this demonstrate the closeness of a new-born baby to God, like Adam before his eviction from the Garden of Eden, for he is still linked to Spirit. It is only when the brain begins to develop along with the emotions, when the powers of discrimination start to grow, when the multifarious influences of the world all around are beginning to be absorbed, that the spiritual level of that child sinks, the spiritual field becomes overlaid with the sensory world of the passions, and spiritual influences are no longer felt.

Growing Physically; Sinking Spiritually

During this period, children are highly vulnerable to bad influences as well as good. It is a simplistic view but an accurate one: before they are in their infant school they will have become little animals, in a truer sense than their parents might suspect. Only a little later, as young teenagers, they will have become filled with the instinctual influences of the plant force – on this descending scale often a turbulent stage in their development as they test their independence.

This is not at all the same as living under the influence of *actual* plants. The instinctual world of plants to which level they have now sunk, on the reverse, occult side of the coin, is a world filled with the red haze of anger, of competition and selfishness. On the surface, it can seem peaceful and alluring, but *no plant can trust another.* It really is the law of the jungle. Like real plants, however, children of this age group have a need for the security of anchoring roots, and an unquestioning readiness to submit to the dominating influence of taller and more arrogant plant-children, and the immovable materiality of adult-objects – the discipline to which as school children and younger siblings they are subject.

Comparatively few people in this day and age, I would hazard a guess, remain permanently on the plant-force level and mature there, to become adult subjects of the Green Man. Older teenagers will already have sunk, on the inner plane, to the level of the material forces. Many, and especially perhaps the more gifted or talented, will have completed their spiritual descent at an earlier age than their peers, a fact which is reflected in their outer lives by the importance they attach to special material skills or possessions. As the learning process continues and intelligence grows, each individual soul normally sinks to a lower and yet lower level, ballasted by the weight of materiality, until virtually the whole human race, in spiritual terms, is approaching rock bottom.

Awareness of Soul Becomes Blotted Out

Like some universal epidemic of encroaching deafness, the whispered advice of Spirit, transmitted by way of the lower soul, which could not only be heard but was listened to constantly by the physically helpless baby, has now become blotted out by the strength of materiality. With ever-increasing insensitivity, the physical movements of the soul become lost beneath the more insistent activity or inactivity brought about by the will. Not only the soul but the body, heart and mind have become enslaved by these material forces – indeed, the body and the brain itself are themselves material objects subject to the laws of materiality. To reverse the process by attempting through one's own efforts to climb back through time and rediscover soul and Spirit, is not as a rule possible.

Theologians have speculated that, alone among historical men, Jesus Christ never grew away from God in this manner but, thanks to the purity of his inheritance (and hence the myth of a virgin birth), and by the grace of his "real" father, remained in the newborn state of close contact with his own soul, able continuously to receive wisdom direct from spiritual realms even during the normal adult development of thoughts and emotions. But there is also the story about the Holy Spirit "descending like a dove" while he was being baptised by John the Baptist – in the same way, perhaps, that the prophet Mohammad received the *Qadr* and, more recently, that Pak Muhammad Subuh received the *Roh Ilofi.* Whatever the truth of the matter, that contact was, and still is, the source of a wisdom that cannot be taught in any human school. He and his soul, being filled with Spirit, were as one. Along with *Sahid Anwar* we must assume that mankind, from the highest to the lowest, were put on earth *in order* to experience and learn from the lower forces as they act upon the inner fabric. It is the only explanation that makes sense. Each individual has perforce to plumb the very depths of materiality before finally commencing the long journey home.

Descending and Ascending Souls

People of the earth who have not fully descended into the material realm may include the wild and innocent tribes of the forest, but they are more likely nowadays to be those quite civilised people who fiercely resist what they may claim to see as the machinations of the devil – or all those features of society that may perhaps be lumped together by some convenient term such as "western degeneracy". These people who do no more than dip their toes fearfully in the sea of experience are the ones who see good in attempting to resist or counter their natural descent, by the whole-hearted adoption of religious fundamentalism . If determined enough, their attitude may mean that they remain stuck, as it were, in the lower realms of instinctual plant forces – still within the fierce power of the Green Man. But let none make the error of supposing that their situation is the same as that of one who has been to the bottom of the spiritual pile and begun to climb back, away from the forces of materiality and up through the decreasingly dense layers of lower forces. *All* the spiritual levels are needed to create an even balance.

With its own momentum, like the swing of a pendulum, a soul can return only to an equal and opposite point no higher than the one it has left. Our common starting point is that of the newborn child – exactly midway in the spiritual hierarchy. No soul can rise to the highest realms unless it first has descended into the depths. Don't forget that "the sinner who repenteth" is better received in heaven than the one who has never put a foot wrong. Even Christ, finally and on the point of death, found himself deserted by the Spirit in common with the rest of mankind and, according to the Christian credo, even his soul was obliged to descend briefly into the material realms of hell before finally ascending to his father's throne.

The Burden of Death

In order to reach the top in spiritual terms, one needs to have experienced the bottom, because a state of wholeness has by definition to include all that is base as well as all that is high. This is why Jesus was obliged to take the burden of human sins upon himself. Apparently, no one expected to go to heaven in Old Testament times, and it makes sense. If people of that time had not yet descended very far below the original human state, they would not be able to rise very far above it when their life on earth was over.

The experience of rising from the heaviest layers of materiality to the lighter realms of the *kejiwaan* is a painful one, for it can only be achieved by way of death, and these heavy forces which have filled our being are unlikely to choose to die voluntarily. This, in practice and in short, is why the path of *Sahid Anwas* can seldom if ever be successful in guiding man's feet up the spiritual track from the lowest satanic forces. A track paved with desire can lead only to the strengthening of those occult influences which hold the soul in thrall, for they *are* desire. Death, by destroying the physical body and with it the will, the sensations, the emotions and the thoughts, is normally the only channel whereby the domination of these lower forces over the soul can be relieved. And in the normal course of events the soul, released on death but unable to rise with its weight of bondage, finds itself drawn again and again towards a recurrent cycle of birth, life and death.

For a person to pursue the course of *Susila Budhi Dharma*, death must come by degrees whilst the body still lives, and whilst the heart and mind still function within their normal environment. It is not particularly pleasant to think about. But, like it or not, when following the *latihan kejiwaan*, that is, when allowing the quickened soul to steer the ship, the human soul has to accept death, for this death is the death of soul contents; death of the passions as they affect mankind. *Susila Budhi Dharma* is indeed "the way of death".

Need to Re-open a Spiritual Channel

"Passions", even satanic ones, cannot of themselves be evil. Indeed, they are essential for the life of the world. Without them, without *desires*, there could be no material universe as we know it, and no creatures able to inhabit it, no forest and no trees, no plants and no flowers. Conservation and good stewardship of the earth pertain to the passions, for the passions dwell within natural life forces. Without passions, there could be no bodily life for humans, no heart and no emotions, no brain and no thoughts. There could also be no enterprise and no attainment. If nature is on the decline, it is because we are abusing these natural life forces, and not the other way round. The important thing for us and for them is to identify the passions, to make oneself familiar with their nature, in order to recognise their absence, and be in a position to accept any finer influences that may be available to us from some source higher than our material selves and the material world. The miracle of the *Subud* contact consists in nullifying the effects of these passions so that just such a receiving can come about. It opens a channel, as it were, between soul and Spirit, re-establishing contact between the lower physical, and the higher spiritual soul of man, between the natural instincts of the earth, and their replenishing source.

> Passions are much admired
>> by those who seek to carve a nook
> In life's symbolic Mount Rushmore of fame,
> Or merit a fine paragraph
>> in the world's great book,
> Or seek to please those
>> who would raise them to acclaim.
>
> One would think to own a passion
>> were a good and noble thing,
> But it has a hindering effect upon the soul;
> For the soul aspires to climb,
>> free of passion's hampering.
> The heart and mind may benefit,
>> but a person should be whole.
>
> Whole: body, heart and mind and soul,
>> are what is termed gestalt,
> Because they add to more than would appear;
> So we often fail to realise
>> what constitutes assault,
> When the parts of us we glorify
>> create the soul's nadir!
>
> Thus have I learnt through life's affairs,
>> through looking inwardly,
> That the passions overcome the helpless soul
> And hold it just as surely
>> as if nailèd to a tree,
> And the nature of the passion
>> is the thing that takes control!

3: THE CYCLE OF NATURE

Reincarnation: Fact or Fiction?

> Some wise men say:
> There is one life, one universe.
> But others, just as wise may say:
> No, there are many; we have countless lives.
> As the galaxies hold countless stars
> so are there countless worlds of men.
>
> Both speak the truth.
> The one who speaks lives once and dies.
> The one who lives and listens and gives power of speech
> lives on forever.

Saving the planet, greening the earth, making the desert flourish; it seems to me that these apparently unselfish aims rest on the assumption of a continuation of plant and animal life forms under the guise of recycled resources. In abstract terms, they rest on the assumption that reincarnation within nature is normal and desirable. On a plant level life is plainly a continual cycle. In the animal world, life seems to be held in scant respect by the creatures that enjoy it. In plain human terms, if animal life were sacred in the sense that we believe our own lives to be sacred, the creator of a world in which creatures are obliged to kill and eat one another in order to live, would have to be a criminal lunatic. Nature runs on instincts and uncaring consequences. Common sense tells us that reincarnation is the "normal" condition of nature.

Paradoxically however, the awakening, the greening of the soul, the discovery of a spiritual green child within, *should* lead, not to an eternity of recycling on an ever-greener planet, but to an end of human recycling. From our own point of view, it should lead to a new and previously unknown stage of existence: the soul must come to conscious awareness. Gradually I have come to the understanding that for humans to accept the occult truth of bodily reincarnation as applying to themselves is to deny spirituality; to accept spirituality on the other hand is to deny reincarnation. The Hindu Vedas certainly bear this out, despite the apparent beliefs and expectations of the majority of Hindus:

The mind that flits like a butterfly through the garden of desires, sipping here and there and caring not for the future, flies to life and death again in the never ending cycle of nature.

A caterpillar, coming to the end of its leaf, reaches across and gains another leaf. The soul, leaving one body behind, reaches across and gains another body.

There are three great powers in nature, created to govern the minerals, the plants, and the animals. When the soul of man is governed also by these powers, he strays blindly along the paths of illusion, wandering endlessly from death to death.

Reincarnation Affecting Souls Untouched by Spirit

As a practical representative of the truth beyond all religions, the international organisation of *Subud* accepts aspirants from any religion or none. When asked by a puzzled Buddhist exactly "where does *Subud* stand with regard to reincarnation?", Pak Subuh explained that "reincarnation is what happens to people who do not follow the *latihan kejiwaan*", that is, whose souls are not outwardly conscious. Those religions which are basically *Anwar* in intent do not acknowledge reincarnation because, rightly or wrongly, their practtitioners believe that to follow the teachings of the founder is to avoid that particular fate. Reincarnation, in fact, is something that normally applies only to those whose souls have not been touched by Spirit.

If this is true, it becomes very obvious why it is so difficult to learn anything very meaningful about reincarnation, because while it applies, the part, or organ or essence of a person which is subject to reincarnation is necessarily unconscious and unable to communicate. But if and when that part, or organ or essence does become conscious, through accident or design, then the process, being no longer operative, is no longer available to be understood. In any case, from our lowly, earthly position within the thrall of instinctual forces which were probably never intended to guide us, it seems impossible even to guess in what part, or organ or essence could reside that continuing flow of personal consciousness that survives between life and life.

We are only too well aware that the physical body and its sensations, the heart and its feelings, the brain and its thoughts, its memories, become abruptly terminated and their value apparently annulled at death. A *bodhisattva* or other advanced aspirant to Buddha status is supposed (and many others have claimed) to have the ability to acquire knowledge of their "previous lives", and of recent years much has been made of apparent regression under hypnosis, during which the subject is taken back in memory, supposedly to a point before conception, before previous death. Numerous people, too, including myself, have experienced vivid dreams of unknown but completely believable and detailed personal lives, consciously experienced in other times and at other places. There may be no doubt that these other lives really happened and such a dream is perfectly genuine, but reincarnation may not necessarily be the key. If you experienced some traumatic incident as a child, for instance, you may well find that all the circumstances surrounding that incident stand out vividly in your memory although the routine of your life at that age has been completely forgotten. Incidents of this kind, in my view, can be 'remembered' quite unexpectedly, perhaps by complete strangers. They constitute the 'memories' of other lives that can be picked up by sensitive dreamers.

World Beliefs and Life After Death

Racial and local variations on the theme of reincarnation abound, and a belief in ghosts, as disembodied souls, is equally widespread, so which are true? Even the most widely differing expectations of various races about their prospects after death do seem to be fulfilled in practice. The belief that the soul of a dead man lives on in his children is prevalent in pagan Africa, and the evidence of it can be observed as the orphaned child (usually the eldest) takes on the psychic purpose and concerns of the dead parent. I have seen it myself, and heard a young African boy speak with his dead father's words, expressing adult views whilst assuming control as head of the family. To tribal Africans it is accepted as normal and greeted with reassurance; but, funnily enough, it never seems to happen to people who do not *believe* in it. My poem *The Garden of God* describes the process of soul-possession in practice:

> Madala withered and stooped and filled with pain
> parched as desert thorns.
> Where, Madala, is your eldest son?
> Your son is a man who gambles and drinks.
>
> Where, Madala, is the soul which honours his mother
> his dark eyes reflecting her
> reflecting her face with the light in his eyes.
> Madala can search in vain with his fading sight.
>
> Madala the child saw the bushland alive with game,
> where now is your eldest son?
> The forest spirits murmur perplexed
> seeing only Madala searching in vain.
>
> Madala, your youngest wife has given birth
> a child daughter dark as evening.
> The eagle owl watched as she was born
> Pure and fresh as carried water.
>
> She stirs the tree roots, Madala, and brings fruit
> and the forest enfolds her to you.
> Her dark eyes reflect you, Madala, one soul,
> filled with life as trees heavy with fruit and honey.
>
> You are once more a child, Madala,
> your two souls are one as the forest flourishes
> as a well-watered garden to nourish you,
> and the garden of God shall bear a new flower.

Probably the most widely held worldwide belief concerning reincarnation supports the idea of a personal line of rebirth through time: "I may be Fred Smith now, but I know that I was once Oliver Cromwell!" This is patently absurd, since Oliver himself was the only real Oliver Cromwell. Fred may have been experiencing something of Oliver's life, but if Oliver actually was the future Fred Smith, did he but know it, who then is Fred now, in reality? Presumably we have all descended from the same spark of life; we are all "I", we are all "me", and if we have that particular ability we may experience other personalities. We are all unique and yet, as can be experienced in the reality of *Susila Budhi Dharma*, we are all one, with a common base in Spirit.

What Part of Me Lives On After Death?

Rank and file Buddhists, by tradition, are constantly aware of the ceaseless round of birth and death, in the context of reincarnation of the individual: life after material life recurring within the earthly time scale, until that particular individual finds eventual enlightenment, as a natural progression towards the scarcely considered resting place of *nirvana*. But simplistic belief in reincarnation tends to leave unanswered the major question: Who am I when I dream? Who was that person, that he or she, that other "I" who has lived before? You may remember a thousand lives, but they are not "your" lives. Every person is unique as an individual, and the centre of his or her own universe. Indeed, one can scarcely deny that we are all "me", as waves are all "sea".

Suppose the concept of personal reincarnation to be literally true, such a state would at least hold out some hope for the world and its inhabitants; the possibility of climbing by degrees. As a vague background belief, it provides the basis for morality and justice. But when pursued more deeply as an intellectual concept, the doctrine of reincarnation is forever bedevilled by the same old questions: Who or what, exactly, becomes reborn again and again? What part of *me* is supposed to learn from this entirely unconscious process? How can *I* amend this ceaseless round? And of course, whilst the process remains an unconscious one, there can be no firm answers. Modern man at any rate seems inclined rather to "self improvement" than to any kind of cessation. Most western Buddhists and Buddhist-style thinkers certainly seem to show more enthusiasm for the prospect of rebirth on earth, than for any hope of final extinction, which for many may seem to have no appeal at all. And this attitude is by no means limited to the pragmatic, intellectual western viewpoint.

The Fate of the Disembodied Soul

It seems clear that the lower human soul, the *sukma*, released on death, follows the cultural expectations which have always filled it during life. Without the guidance of Spirit, if it has accepted any belief unquestioningly during life, unconsciously it will be drawn towards the fulfilment of that belief. If during life it had no such belief, it will be obliged to wander, seeking a new home. The Svetasvatara Upanishad expresses it in poetic terms:

In a dream a wise man saw the river of life rushing in full spate, flowing from a fountain of consciousness; fed by five turbid tributaries of the senses, with high waves whipped up by the winds of passionate breath; with five great whirlpools full of sorrow and loneliness, and five rocky ravines echoing with danger and pain.

Along the turgid river of life flies a solitary swan with whistling wings — the human soul seeking quiet waters on which to rest. While she flies with a restless heart she despairs of finding peace; but when Spirit guides she is shown a tranquil lake with clear water and sheltering reeds.

An Encounter Between Soul and Spirit

So, what is the personal link with this most uncommon common base? The lower personal soul, the *sukma,* can by chance or by way of occult practices, or even by the use of drugs, become known and vividly experienced within the compass of the material forces, apparently quite without the benefit of higher spiritual contact. Many conclusions may be drawn from this apparent knowledge.

But without doubt it is the higher, impersonal human soul, known by practitioners of *Subud* as the *Jiwa*, which stands above the worldly life forces, above the workings of materiality, and above the instincts of plants, animals and men within the cycle of nature; the Spirit that can normally be experienced directly only after the death of the physical body.

The point I would like to make is this: the quickened lower soul, as the *sukma*, seems to have no recollection of "previous lives" though it is filled with personal contents some of which may have been acquired before birth. Higher soul, as *Jiwa* — the impersonal Spirit, has no personal contents in this way. Spirit is not personal and particular, and is not bound by humanity, high or low. The more awake, the more conscious the inner self becomes, the more hazily does reincarnation recede.

Buddhists in particular have always been acutely aware in their teachings and traditions of the natural human condition that is operative while the unconscious soul remains captive within earthly life forces — materiality as distinct from materialism — a continual blanket process of reincarnation; caught up in nature with a constant succession of "I's". Gurdjieff's Fourth Way aimed to reduce the number of "I's" to one. It would seem that there is never a time when "I am not". The burning question posed by Hindus and pursued by Buddhists is: "How can the knower be known?", which leads one on to ask: How can the one within who says "I am", himself be known for what he (or she) truly is?

An Introduction to Spirit

The earliest Buddhist doctrine stressed the impersonal nature of the higher spiritual "self", and warned against the evidently almost inescapable folly of not being able to accept one's own higher self when the time comes — the self that alone can lift the individual human being above the "net of reincarnation, cast about the earth". The very ancient *Tibetan Book of the Dead* described an encounter with Spirit at the moment of death:

Swifter than lightning, the splendour of the pure white light of emptiness will make its appearance, and surround you on all sides. Terror may seize you, and wishing to escape you may lose consciousness. Try to accept that light! Give up your illusions, your belief in a personal worldly self. Only recognise that this light is your own true self, the boundless reality, and you shall be saved!

Perhaps the best way to avoid the trauma of such a sudden confrontation is to take part in some kind of process of gradual introduction to Spirit — an ever-increasing exposure of the lower soul and the ego-oriented worldly self, to that "boundless reality" of the true self. The Subud contact is supposed to initiate exactly that. It is axiomatic that the way to spiritual life is by the way of physical death. Exposure to Spirit through this contact brings about the "spiritual movement" known as the *latihan kejiwaan*, which by inducing a progressive if temporary paralysis of the passions, in effect causes the spiritual processes of death actually to take place during physical life.

An ancient Zen master once said: "Men are afraid to stop thinking for fear of falling through the void. But that void is the true realm of the dharma. As it cannot be sought with the mind, it cannot be understood, or explained, or touched. It cannot be taken by force or won through good works. Yet it is still ourselves". Whether we call it stillness or void, it is only by way of that cessation of passions that we can open the *sukma*, and commence the process of spiritual purification.

Thoughts and Feelings as a Hindrance

For the mind deliberately to attempt to let go of itself is to lose spontaneity and introduce artificiality. Neither mind nor no-mind can be grasped with the mind, but "when spring comes, the new grass grows by itself". It is not easy for sophisticated minds to arrive at the conclusion that, if only temporarily, thinking is no longer of use, and even harder for the wilful human heart to accept that the feelings must be allowed to stand to one side to make room for understanding. The function of emotion, symbolised by the heart, is to make value judgements, and through our hearts we like to feel important. In this case the heart must do no more than watch and listen; value judgements can come later.

From whichever direction one approaches the necessity of submission to higher, spiritual powers, one must arrive at the same conclusion. It is not a case of locating and strengthening something that you already have; not a case of finding some formula or technique that will bring "positive results"; of creating this, that, or the other in yourself: it *cannot be done* by *Anwas* means. The passions themselves, these driving motives, the instinctive clinging to life which characterises physical existence, preclude the possibility of submission to anything not of their nature, and are themselves the cause of the "terror" described in the ancient Tibetan tradition. Fear is a peculiarity of the heart, and the heart is the scat of the passions. With hindsight, fear of Spirit could explain the strange undercurrent of opposition that occurs whenever a person working "from the inner" tries to do something really practical. In retrospect one can see that opposition to *Anwar* solutions arises from the aggrieved passions fearing for their own welfare, voiced through the minds of otherwise well-meaning people. From experience, one can see that distrustful obstruction will cease only when a truly significant proportion of influential people actually achieve submissive contact with Spirit, and in more specific terms, pursue the *latihan kejiwaan* of *Subud*.

Fear of the Spiritual Unknown

It is quite normal for the heart to feel fear when confronted with spiritual phenomena: it seems to come as a threat to emotional status. But fear of the spiritual unknown marks the point at which a major breakthrough – a miraculous event – is needed. To understand "what" and "why" is comparatively easy. Only the good fortune of an introduction to Spirit (in practice perhaps, an introduction to *Subud*), can provide an answer to the far more important question: "how?" By clearing a way through the passions and stopping their influence at the crucial moment of contact and beyond, the *latihan kejiwaan* of *Subud*, being a spiritual exercise that is free from the outside influence of the passions, eliminates fear of Spirit, and removes the old bug-bear of instinctive opposition to submissive solutions. Where there is no *nafsu* there is no fear.

Repeated many times at regular intervals, the process of the *latihan* is able gradually to raise the status of individuals from their previous rating in the universal spiritual hierarchy (however lowly that status may be), to improve their fate and modify their karma. Through sincere submission to the recurrent experience of subtle death, it becomes possible at last to escape the binding power of mortality and thereby, purely incidentally, be admitted to the non-material secrets of life on earth, and the life of the earth.

A New Spiritual Centre of Gravity

For anyone who sincerely follows the *latihan kejiwaan* of *Subud*, though it may be only after many years that the perception arises, the subtle spiritual functioning of birth and death takes on a clearly recognisable form reflecting the innermost workings of karmic processes: a succession of differing but equally personal "souls", a succession of lives within a life. As one soul, one sukma, seems to die, it is in order that it can gradually be replaced by a newly born centre of gravity, a new personal level of being that much further from one's old pre-*Subud* self, and that much nearer, so the conviction grows, to God. At the same time the individual may well have observed a procession of passing "obsessions", or interests, or eccentricities, each lasting perhaps weeks, perhaps months, perhaps years, interests that one might suppose to have formed the basis each of a separate life in a new body, under the unseen karmic rules of reincarnation: each of these passing interests has the potential of a new birth, a new ego, a new heart, a new brain, a new set of perceptions. In the normal way – the way of unconsciousness – it is a case of "one soul, one life"; and this, so it seems to me, is the cardinal principle of reincarnation. To become aware of it in this way is to escape from it.

The innermost individual self comes consciously to embrace the outermost non-individual self – this is more or less the working of the collective unconscious of Jung's understanding – and at the very moment when the thinking mind and the feeling heart are completely quiet, the aspirant may experience all that his fellows experience. Independently of his thinking he may become instantaneously aware of their personal contents as well as his own. Against his will he is forced to the conclusion that all men are indeed one. As it is the rule for men and women to conduct their own *latihan* separately, I can present only the male point of view from personal experience. Women following this spiritual exercise may or may not have different perceptions, but certainly both the male and the female soul is moved as Spirit wills and, though different, both are equal in the *kejiwaan,* in the field of Spirit.

Changing Levels of Understanding

Both male and female followers of this spiritual exercise are, by and large, practical people who usually care little for theories or symbols. But though few of them may be interested in probing and analysing and weighing their own contents, through their own gradual progress they cannot help but discover for themselves that their own level of perception, of understanding, constantly changes. In the great scheme of things one perceives that it is not so much deeds or principles that have levels of quality, as the people who react to them. What may have seemed quite out of the question a few years back, they discover, may seem quite in order now. Later, when their perceptions have again changed, it may well seem undesirable again – and of course the opposite will equally well apply.

This phenomenon itself is the experience of *satori* at a level undreamed of in Zen, repeated over and over at ever ascending degrees. Through this process of inner *satori,* one is set on an upward course to climb through successive layers of perception. To take an example of changing perceptions, blasphemy can seem very worrying to one whom we shall call a middle-religious person. It can be a highly emotional matter, and reaction to it may even involve violence and murder. To a pre-religious person the principle of blasphemy is quite beyond understanding – a simple matter of arbitrary rules to be kept or broken at will. To an anti-religious rebel, blasphemy may seem a calculated act of defiance, like the child who punishes God by refusing to believe in Him. To one whom we shall call a post-religious person, blasphemy as such can scarcely exist. It will be seen as a potential offence against the feelings of the individual who hears it, rather than an offence against Almighty God, whose mind and whose feelings would have to be as broad and all-encompassing as his universe. It is passion alone – everyday self within the limits of materiality – that is affected, and the people who live within the limits of the passions who are influenced by such matters as blasphemy. The irony, in my view, is that the passions themselves have the nature of forming a barrier between God and man, between the spiritual and the profane.

Awakening : the Birth of a Spiritual Child

Sudden awakening, whether it be a once-only affair or, as in this case, an ongoing experience, has its religious counterparts in the Christian experience of being "born again", and in the Islamic experience of the *Qadr* that is said to descend upon the faithful during their Ramadan fast. It also follows the partial awakening brought about by entering the second intuitional phase of the astrological threefold cycle at the age of twenty eight. It cannot be thought of as merely an intuitional, or an emotional and certainly not an intellectual change of perception, though all of these functions will certainly be involved. Human imagination – another product of materiality – is always ready to modify or falsify events, unless it can somehow be set aside and temporarily abandoned. The "opening" experienced by followers of the spiritual *latihan* of *Subud*, at the very start of their purifying process, is exactly this hoped-for and long-awaited experience: the birth of the green child, the commencement of a journey beyond materiality, with the least likelihood of imagination being allowed to participate.

Perfect awakening, when it takes place at all on this earth, takes place at once, within the context of everyday life — that is, before any process of "spiritual purification" has even commenced. If it had to wait for spiritual purification to take place first, it could never happen, because the one depends on the other, the purification follows from the opening. It has never, therefore, been an experience limited to the "pure in heart", or exclusively a reward for a lifetime of dedication, though this is not to say that it might not also *be* such a reward. In religious terms, rebirth is something that occurs at a definite time and place. At the outset of *Susila Budhi Dharma*, far from being a once-for-all experience, having occurred it continues to function automatically and indefinitely as a permanent state of being whilst the recipient goes about his or her daily round.

Passions of Nature Acting as a Barrier

So, one might reason, without the aid of "organisations" of any kind, having summarised and understood the problem and formulated the solution, why can one not simply "be still" in the spirit of the psalm, and "receive" the movement of one's own soul? After all, Spirit is not owned, as a commodity to be dispensed. Now the "technique" is known, why not just do it yourself? The short answer is: it won't work. The passions of nature will not be persuaded to give way; your "receiving" will be yet another product of those passions, lacking the collective human channel — a clear passageway through the inner selves of others who have already been "opened". People have always tried to isolate themselves from worldly passions through lives of abstinence and austerity. Some may even have succeeded in these aims, who can tell? But centuries ago worldly influences, I am sure, were less insistent than they are today, particularly in countries which encouraged the religious hermit. Could any of us today take Shantideva's 8th century poem to heart and live a totally reclusive life like the *bodhisattva* in his poem, without any of the benefits of civilisation?

Alone and unknown shall I dwell,
In peace and with untroubled mind,
Like the new moon will I live my hidden life.

Fain would I dwell in the forest,
Beneath a tree, or in a cave,
In disregard for all, ne'er looking back.

Trees show me no disdain,
And trees demand no tiresome wooing:
Fain would I welcome them as companions.

Fain would I dwell 'midst leafy rocks
Owned by no man,
And there, a hermit, follow my own mind.

Reclusive Attitudes No Longer Appropriate

Today, a hermit monk's life would probably seem selfish and rather useless. It is simply not compatible with the healthy continuing life of humankind on earth. And strongest of all arguments against it, there is simply no *need* nowadays to withdraw to a life of solitude in monastery or leafy hermitage. There is no need for meditation or ritual; no need for austerities of the body, denials of the heart, or tricks of the mind. There is certainly no need for any arrogant assumption of "spirituality"; no need to avoid good business practices. It is said we have two obligations in the eyes of the Almighty: to manage the earth and our personal and family affairs efficiently; and, by accepting Spirit, to submit our inner selves into God's hands. It is not a case of "either-or". The two may seem irreconcilable simply because of the passions involved in the first obligation. These passions cannot be eliminated, because their elimination would entail our own physical death; but neither should they be permitted to flourish unrestrained at the "opening" of *Subud* or during the *latihan kejiwaan*. They are simply required to come to rest, whilst we neither indulge them nor struggle against them.

If one looks for explanations of the mechanics of all this before the event, one cannot do better than to look within the Buddhist context. After the event there will be the plentiful explanations given by Pak Subuh Sumohadiwidjojo, but these are not to be read or listened to before the experience itself. To take them as yet more theories would be unfortunate; the practice of *Subud* is not something to be weighed up and judged: the spiritual exercise is an exercise of the soul and is not intended for the brain. The brain cannot venture far beyond the material, but we can safely return to religious explanations, particularly those of the Buddha himself.

Whether he is seen now as the historical sage Shakyamuni, or as one of the mythical superman heroes of Mahayana tradition, in breaking away from the multiplicity of gods each representing a fragment of reality, the Buddha recognised and depicted these divisions of power as fragmentations already existing within the self. But as manifestations of the passions, they were to be looked upon as illusions to be dispelled rather than as parts of the whole to be reunited, or as rungs of a ladder waiting to be climbed. There was no "climbing" for the Buddha. Man's highest potential he saw as pre-existent and attainable, provided all else could be ignored as the illusory *samsara*.

A Rebirth to be Avoided

"If gods exist," Buddha said, "they must be subject to the same laws as all else". And of course, as the gods were personifications of the passions of nature, they must fall under natural laws. But for ordinary men and women, the universal forces and base passions and instincts that order the lives of all worldly creatures and maintain the balance of nature – these gods – could be ignored only at one's peril. *The Tibetan Book of the Dead* includes dramatic descriptions of the major life forces when they are seen as spiritual levels of being, as places of possible rebirth for any human soul with the misfortune to fall under their sway:

"I am dead!" exclaims your disembodied soul. "What shall I do?" You will feel as anguished as a fish on hot coals. Having no sense objects on which to rest, your consciousness will be wafted like a feather on the breeze. Then the furious wind of karma will rise and blow you helplessly along with fearful gusts.

"What would I not give, to possess a body!" You will find no place to hide, no safe place to enter except the crevices of rocks and boulders into which you are blown, and to which you vainly cling. Then will shine upon you the coloured lights of the six places of rebirth. Your own karma will decide which light shines the brightest, which place will attract you by its colour as a place in which to be reborn. This light will seem soothing to you and you will be drawn towards it.

If past good deeds have merited it, a white light will guide you to one of the heavens, where you will find happiness for a while among the gods. Past habits of envy and ambition will guide you to a red light, which as you enter it leads to the fierce world of the Asuras; forever agitated with anger. If you feel drawn towards a blue light, you will be reborn a human being in this land of hardship and unhappiness. If the green light attracts you, you will find yourself in the dull world of animals, excluded from the knowledge that brings salvation. A hazy yellow light leads to the nebulous world of ghosts, and a smoky grey light leads to the hells below the earth. Be not afraid! View them all with complacency. Remember that these visions are unreal. You alone are the source of these lights. You alone are the source of the dark worlds into which they lead.

I can scarcely resist reiterating this excerpt in poetic terms:

> The disembodied soul
> Tibetans say
> is shown
> a blinding light
> surrounding itself on all sides:
> *seeing the light;*
> the brilliance of the higher self,
> radiance of spirit
> from which
> in ignorance
> the soul may shrink in terror.

And shrinking from that awesome light
the soul alone
and helpless
finds itself caught up by winds –
fierce winds of karma
blowing the souls of men
amongst the fractured elements.

Shorn of reassuring corporality,
bereft of senses and solidity
the soul is hurled and whirled
struggling and gibbering
terror stricken
amongst material elements
ungraspable.

Its only hope to cling
and hide
in crevices within the rock
– rock of the world's materiality in subtle guise –
until it finds itself within a cave,
a respite from the winds of fate
and karmic consequence.

And in that sheltering cave
five lesser caves
with lesser lights
less terrifying than that first blinding light,
shining with colours
that may attract
and soothe the frightened soul.

The colour that the soul may choose
decides its destiny,
its next rebirth,
so the Tibetans say.
A red light
red as glowing coals
marking the entrance to a cave:

THE CYCLE OF NATURE

A passageway which leads
the unsuspecting soul
attracted by that savage glow
into a world of strife and violence
of arrogance and envy
enticing and enfolding souls
whose vengeful passions
live on after death:
within the subtle world of plants.

A green light
shining from another cave:
another passageway which leads
the soul attracted by that light
into a world which to some might seem
a peaceful verdant place,
but this is a world bereft of reason
excluded from the wisdom
that redeems mankind,
a world of death
and birth and death again,
within the kingdom of the beasts.

A blue light
soothing to most peaceful souls
shines from the next cave
luring people to rebirth
within this world of men,
and life with all its joys and sorrows
ending in rebirth to live and die again,
for souls still shunning that bright radiance
that promises escape
from this
the multi-coloured world of nature,
encountered from within.

A smoky murky light
Tibetans say
leads to the hells beneath the earth
– a fearsome place best not described.

A nebulous yellow glow as well
may still attract the soul
unwilling to commit to nature's world
of corporality,
unwilling to submit to change:
this cloudy yellow light leads to the land of ghosts.

One small redeeming chance remains
an option for the soul who shunned the light
and radiance of immortal spirit:
There is a lesser light, a pure white light,
that may be seen and seized by those
who spurned the caverns of rebirth;
if good deeds in this life have merited
a brief reward,
the light of sensual paradise
– an echo of earth's transient joys –
a place of carnal lust and food and drink
that lasts as long as passions live on after death.

But as the earthly passions fade and die forever
so will such a temporal paradise dissolve
and blow away once more
scattered by those karmic winds
dispersed into the elements.
So the Tibetans say.
And be it known, the burden of their message
has to be:
we all must die,
we all may see that blinding light:
accept that radiant light with open arms –
it is thine own true self!

An Inside View of the Forces of Nature

The descriptions of the places of rebirth in *The Tibetan Book of the Dead,* dating back several thousand years, were certainly based on instinctive human knowledge, on *dhyana*: soul without Spirit, relating to the knowledge of the *sukma* as distinct from *Jiwa;* the end product of Zen as distinct from that of *Susila Budhi Dharma.*

110

Advanced devotees of *Anwar* today, similarly bereft of Spirit (the common state of mankind) but finally in touch with their own "truly human" instinct, and thus perhaps having regained something of Stone Age man's intuitive perceptions, come to a very similar understanding. An understanding, that is, of the differing levels of being into which rebirth is possible, whether one's physical death intervenes or not. The "lights of the places of rebirth" describe the disembodied soul's view of the instinctual life forces that govern the world and its materiality – the light essence of minerals, plants, animals, the ordinary nature-bound humans, and beyond. Though it may seem to vary according to cultural expectations and the individual capacity to perceive it (Stone Age caves, rocks and crevices may have become modern rooms and buildings!), it is the same intuitive understanding that has come to sages, saints and seekers of many varied cultures in past ages.

The question posed by the *Jiwa* might be: "Are you master or slave? Are you subordinate to those essential forces, or are they subordinate to you?" The outcome will depend upon the instinctive answer. The celebrated 13th century Sufi, Jalal-uddin Rumi, wrote: "As a mineral I died and became a plant. As a plant I died and became an animal. As an animal I died and I was a man. Why should I fear? When was I less by dying? As a man I shall die, to soar with the blessed angels; but even from angelhood I must pass on. All except God perishes. When I have sacrificed my angel soul, I shall become that which no mind ever conceived."

The quotation suggests that medieval Sufis tended to have strangely literal minds. But whether taken as concrete realities or as mere abstractions, all these levels of being in their subtle nature make up the structure of the inner self. People in whom the *kejiwaan* is a reality may or may not acknowledge this, and it can matter little either way, for as they are well aware, there is no need to believe or disbelieve, or to analyse any part of it. But when such people – those of the *Anwar* persuasion – do accept these levels of being, they go further than *Sahid Anwas*; they see the self as filled and surrounded by different life forces, some of which are by

111

nature below, others above the truly human level of being. One's view of the self is the same as one's view of the earth. Their situation and their needs are so similar as to be indistinguishable. Once spiritual deterioration has set in, the contents of either may be revivified only through the intervention of higher, finer, non-self, non-material influences.

The Structure of the Inner Self

It has become very plain that the age-old comparison between self and not-self has been irrelevant all along. Theories about spiritual matters may have interest, but they count for nothing in practical terms. When one's understanding of such matters is based upon actual experience, as all real understanding must be, one invariably comes to realise that, whilst experiencing the ever-changing levels of spirituality, whilst imbibing them, one's self remains quite separate and distinct from these subtle forces. At the same time, however, and paradoxically, they are still part of the person, the contents of one's own soul, and to disown them must inevitably involve an unnecessary risk.

Perhaps I should apologise for returning once again to the *Tibetan Book of the Dead*, however fascinating it is, for there is really no need to raise the ghost of ancient writings in an attempt to give weight to experiences that are freely available today. The only criterion is personal experience. My excuse is the inevitability of death, for: "Unless you find it in this life, you will find it in no other". And so let us look again at that ancient work's description of the soul's experience immediately following the moment of death. The very first perception that strikes the mirror of the soul is a reflection of the highest – that flash of blinding light, the pure white light of Spirit that occupies all voids. Spirit precedes and accompanies all creations. It surrounds you and fills you, for it is the impersonal spiritual essence of your own true self. The human heart feels fear when confronted with true spirituality. But to accept that light as you are at that time, bereft of intellect and emotion, is to allow yourself to be merged within its radiance.

112

Escaping the Influence of Lower Forces

"You alone are the source of these dark worlds", but the act of accepting the terrifyingly pure light of Spirit as "your own true self" serves to overcome their power. To the ancient Buddhist it was self-evident that the self was not only surrounded by these lower forces, but it too surrounded them. By ceasing to be influenced by them, through acceptance of Spirit, it became possible to embrace them fearlessly in that boundless reality which is the familiar soul of man, *being filled with Spirit.* By being filled with Spirit, the soul exceeds the bounds of personality, embraces and becomes one with the greater, impersonal soul that is above all dark worlds of becoming.

The base passions, earthly desires, are the stuff of these same universal forces whilst they exert their influence over man's psyche. Seen in the reflected light of Spirit, combined, they form the natural instinctual urges that direct the living world and its creatures in an orderly fashion, maintaining the balance or deciding the imbalance of nature, comprising the sum of countless individual karmic behaviour patterns working together as a multi-structured life force. Things remain mere things. Plants remain mere plants. Animals remain mere animals. Humans alone, having dominion over beasts in the biblical sense, as the fourth above the triad, are able consciously or unconsciously to feel the flow of these forces as a power for good or evil. The ability to feel this power and make good use of it in this scientific age is an end worth pursuing – but it must *not* become a "passion" in itself.

The Effect of Inappropriate Influences

I have already tried to describe some of the effects that the plant life forces can have on human nature. Even individual plants can fill a person with their own essence, simply by being eaten or used in other ways, when "passion" is involved. In these days of the supermarket such influences are less obvious that once was the case, but are that much more complex. In peasant communities, plant-characters are far more obvious, with readily identifiable potato people, wheat people, rice people. Then there are bamboo people, and pine people, and tree influence is not confined to the unsophisticated. In the western sawmills even now we can meet the taciturn and strangely unyielding oak people.

Animal influence is even more marked. Anyone with a "sensitive eye" will have noted the more obvious cases of animal character and appearance making itself known within the human individual, where inappropriate forces have been allowed inadvertently to exert their dominance. There is the over-concerned pet owner who begins to look like his or her pet; there are the numerous people who show in their features, their habits and their physique, obsessive animal loves and cruelties (both imply excessive influence involuntarily exerting itself) deeply seated within themselves, their parents and their children. There are horse people, camel people, cat people, dog people, cow, sheep, pig, poultry and pheasant people, insect people, snail people. It is often a sort of unspoken joke – for instance in the widespread rural superstition about a pregnant mother having been "frightened by" whatever it may be that has made its influence known. We may not "believe" it, but we all know in our hearts that this type of influence is very real.

It is chiefly when the life forms of other species involve strong feelings, when there is attraction or revulsion, that their subtle forms take on tangible shape. But this is merely the tip of an iceberg. Such unseen influence is normally far greater than the outward appearances suggest; and it does not necessarily require any heavy-handed interference with the laws of nature, or an obsessive interest in particular animals, plants or material wealth, to trigger these subtle effects on the driving force of the individual. They are widespread and deep-reaching. So much of everyday human behaviour mirrors the nature of life forces which originate below the level of the true nature of mankind as they exert this unsuspected and quite involuntary influence on the receptive part of human nature.

114

A World-Embracing Mantle of Power

It makes more sense if you consider all this as deriving from a world-embracing mantle of power which has the full range of possibilities, all natural actions and attitudes, woven into its fabric; the ebb and flow of vibrations or waves of instinct. As the impulse ruling the animal kingdom, these vibrations direct impartially the lifestyles of the whale and the hyena, determine the migration of birds, the teeming world of insects. Such forces guide the lion to ambush the zebra; equally they guide the zebra to evade the lion, and are therefore constantly in a state of tension, filled equally with the possibilities of both triumph and defeat. Man is also said to be an animal, and as such is subject to the urges of the animal world: in striving to keep a balance within the whole, these instincts can bestow an insatiable desire for sex. And to ensure that this end is capable of being fulfilled, they can be a source of boundless energy, arrogance, bravery, possessiveness, selfishness; also of bluff, caution, cowardice and pride, patriotism and ambition. But "all flesh is grass", and man also has the life forces of the plant world to contend with – the sum total, that is, of countless distinctive patterns of growth, and almost as many instinctual, impersonal methods of reproduction, ranging from indiscriminate pollination to highly complex individual specialisations.

The Inner World of Plants

Within the hidden mantle of power are contained the urges and the means for individual life forms to behave perhaps like a forest tree, or a cactus, like a seaweed, or even an invisible micro-organism. Changes of vibration within these layers of instinct, if it comes at all, comes slowly, and equally those people influenced by them can change only slowly too, perhaps after a succession of deaths and rebirths. "Plant influence" can be ruthlessly impersonal.

At first glance plants may seem quite serenely peaceful creations: submissive; sweet-natured as a bouquet of flowers. But this is their surface behaviour as we perceive it, and their pace of life is not as fast as ours; their instinctual inner drive belies this calm appearance. Deep down, this is indeed the fierce infra-red world of the titanic *Asuras* perceived by Tibetan Buddhists — a world in which every individual must battle constantly if it is to survive in the face of a hostile environment and ruthless competition; a fight or die world. Although that world is so varied, capabilities are limited. Plants lack the mobility of animals and humans, and no plant can adapt beyond its own preordained uniqueness. A shade-bearer will tolerate the shade of taller plants, a light-demander cannot: there is no compromise. When its limits are challenged it must either overpower the opposition or succumb to it. The welfare of neighbouring plants is not a matter for instinctual concern. A continuous power struggle is in operation within the plant kingdom: each individual plant possesses as it were an inbuilt urge to conquer the world.

An established plant community is an interesting phenomenon with predictable characteristics, well known in differing terms to foresters, farmers and ecologists, but less obvious to most others. An ancient woodland, for instance, is not as it may at first appear a chaotic or haphazard arrangement of forms, but a closely-knit multi-structured community able to function as a unit only through its inter-relating set of instincts: roots feeding at different depths, foliage seeking the sun at differing levels and in differing degree, flowers employing varying modes of reproduction. When the fine equilibrium of this peaceful plant community is disturbed by whatever means, each plant must in effect struggle to win power — to take over all available space. That peaceful community had come about and was maintained only through ruthless and completely selfish competition, the endless striving from a pioneering to a climactic mode of living. And this, in essence, is the quality that "plant influence" lends to the human psyche.

The mysterious, foreboding quality of a forest, filled with this enmity, this tension, held in check by the *status quo*, has often been used to dramatic effect in the world of fiction. Many writers have sensed the powerful passions that lie in wait, eager to be unleashed. Algernon Blackwood described it in his short story *The man whom the trees loved:*

Jealousy was not confined to the human and animal world alone, but ran through all creation. The Vegetable Kingdom knew it too. So-called inanimate nature shared it with the rest. Trees felt it. This Forest just beyond the window – standing there in the silence of the autumn evening across the little lawn – this Forest understood it equally. The remorseless branching power that sought to keep exclusively for itself the thing it loved and needed, spread like a running desire through all its million leaves and stems and roots. In humans, of course, it was consciously directed; in animals it acted with frank instinctiveness; but in trees this jealousy rose in some blind tide of impersonal and unconscious wrath that would sweep opposition from its path as the winds sweep powdered snow from the surface of ice. Their number was a host with endless reinforcements, and once it realised its passion was returned the power increased.

Mineral Instincts – the Forces of Materiality

Coarser than the subtle urgings of the plant, the animal, and the human life forces, more powerful and all-pervasive, are the vibrations of materiality – the "mineral instincts", the physical impulses regulating the behaviour of particles through the laws of physics. The physical body is rightly the province of this material life force; the inner self ought to be free from it, but through its subtle nature it all too readily forms the spiritual centre of gravity in humans too. It may not be readily recognisable for what it is, but when seen in the context of the whole we can appreciate how powerful this "instinct" must be, once it becomes firmly established within the human psyche. It can instil the impulse of greed for personal possessions, but it also provides the desire and the ability to make and build and use, to manufacture ever more complicated tools, to advance in material terms. It follows that the world's more advanced countries and their inhabitants tend to be deeply steeped in this coarse, but still very desirable set of material instincts.

The spiritual consequences of these "lower life forces" have been felt, feared, and described since earliest times, reappearing in many symbolic forms through myth and fable. All the "underworld" myths through the ages abound with personifications of their various aspects. The three-headed dog Cerberus very tellingly represents the three life forces below the truly human level, and he was said to welcome newcomers into Hades with wagging tail, but once inside they were prevented from leaving. The Green Man himself, of course, is no less than a personification of plant force instinct, though he may also represent far more than this. In the Judaic-Christian-Muslim traditions, the material life force in particular, as *roh sjetaniah*, the "satanic force", has been personalised as Satan, the Evil One. In popular myth Satan has been ascribed many and varied forms and functions, but perhaps his place in the world has been nowhere so well understood as in the biblical Book of Job:

Now there was a day when the Sons of God came to present themselves before the Lord, and Satan came also among them. And the Lord said unto Satan, Whence cometh thou? Then Satan answered the Lord, and said, From going to and fro in the earth, and from walking up and down in it.

The Human Life Force Cannot Act Alone

The satanic, the plant, and the animal: these are the three lower life forces which have seemed sometimes to obsess the ancients; but permeating these three there is also the human life force – the original human instinct, the finest and subtlest of patterns in this overall mantle of power. Such instinctual life forces as are appropriate to mankind alone are said to bestow man's ability to discriminate, to observe, and to make balanced judgements. But although this human life force is the most appropriate driving force when it predominates in our lives, it can also give rise to a rather undesirable type of arrogance – the feeling that man is top of the tree, not merely in the material world, but in the entire cosmic order of things. Though it may have been the driving instinct of Eden, the human life force, in other words, has little compatibility

118

with what modern people might consider to be feelings of devotion towards an unknowable Almighty God. It can be the source of god-like inflation: the worship of man and the power of humanity.

People in whom the human life force, as *roh jasmani*, predominates, may feel that they possess reason, but they do not seem to be in possession of *dhyana*. As a personal view again, they do not even seem to be particularly good or pleasant people. Rather, they seem cold and selfish, lacking compassion and humility in a way that brings to mind the biblical account of the pre-flood people whom God saw fit to drown. The plain fact is, if we are to be whole people, we *need* the whole range of "lower forces" operating through us, but in a selective way. One learns through the *latihan kejiwaan* that the soul has separate compartments or "personalities" that operate through and depend upon *all* these natural, instinctual forces. Wholeness can come about only when all these reflective facets of the self can combine into a type of compassion that embraces the world. We cannot evade these lower life forces, nor should we wish to do so. *Anwas* policies aimed at excluding them are quite inappropriate. The cycle of nature can continue apace, correctly channelled from our human viewpoint. From our predominantly material centre of gravity, triggered by Spirit, our need is to climb back up the hill, allowing each of these natural powers to slot into its appropriate place, gradually and eventually to "become again like a little child", at the high-human point of birth. The original descent was a process of fragmentation. Our ascent will be a process of unification, uniting all these life forces into one compassionate focus.

A Universal Mandala

All this presents a complicated view of the self which may be better explained by means of a diagram. The universal mandala overleaf can represent both the "above" and the "below", the spiritual contents both of the world and of the individual. The self can then be considered as an image, a microcosm, at one with the macrocosm of the world:

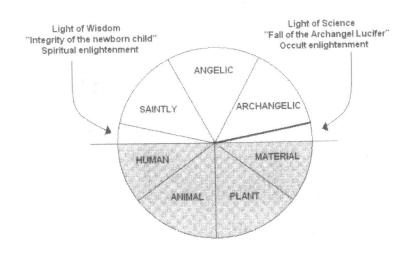

As pictures of the soul, mandalas take many forms. Usually they represent a cycle, a seemingly spinning wheel of apparently connected categories. But there is no accommodation for completely free cycling of the soul, nor could there be. Barriers exist at every division of soul-level. These are the almost invariably misunderstood astrological septile aspects, or "divisions of death", and the mandala can also play the part of an astrological birthchart. On the eastern horizon (by astrological reckoning to the left of the diagram), the new-born child descends from the saintly level of the unborn to the level of ordinary humans. On the western horizon (to the right) the light of Lucifer descends from the archangelic level to the level of the satanic or material force. Both the human and the satanic sections extend a little way above the horizon, and both extremities of the horizon are illuminated by the heavenly light of the spiritual worlds above them. Only the lower worlds of ordinary humans, of animals, of plants, and of material things, are in darkness. Both the new-born child and the occult materialist are bathed equally in the light of wisdom. The natural course of creation runs in a clockwise direction, from the barren world of materiality – the solid sphere of the earth itself – taking in first the plant life forces as the world becomes clothed in greenery, then the animal and finally the human life forces. As the child grows, however, he or she soon leaves the light – the guidance of *Jiwa* – and travels on soul level against the flow of creation, continuing the descent through darker and darker levels of being, through the realms of animal and plant, finally to mature within the satanic sector of materiality.

A universal mandala in this form not only illustrates quite clearly the "underground" influence of the plant and animal worlds, it also makes plainer what I would describe as "encapsulation" of the soul, which can follow immersion in the apparent wisdom of occult practices. The wisdom which the occultist can acquire in this westerly extremity may be real, but it is highly dubious because it holds out false hope. There is no way for a soul finding itself within the satanic realm to rise directly to the archangelic realm above it. Even the Archangel Lucifer himself, after his fall, could not climb back to spiritual realms, though the light of wisdom shining through makes them seem connected. The bulk of humanity, crowded into this material sector, remain trapped. Many feel constrained to climb towards the light, but the lure of "upwards" in this material zone is in fact "downwards" by the occult force of gravity. Individuals may succeed in reaching the light and by doing so they may well have achieved something real in the field of science, but this wisdom is on a par with the occult. It is not the road to heaven. They cannot exceed these occult bounds of the satanic region; they can only immerse themselves ever more deeply in materiality. The only real route of escape involves a somewhat barren journey back through the dark and seemingly unrewarding worlds of plants and animals, finally to regain the truly human point of birth. Only then, having really become again like a little child, is the way open for them to reach the world of saints, and whatever may lie beyond. To recapitulate the great descent in human or historical terms, to understand how the everyday natural desires and ambitions tend to carry the communal and individual soul on a downward journey, we may best look to the poetic description of life's great game of snakes and ladders:

> In Eden (so the fable says)
>   there was a special tree
> And if you ate the fruit of it
>   your heart and mind would be
> Filled with forbidden knowledge,
>   learning, pride and lust as well.
> The crafty serpent tempted Eve
>   and then old Adam ate,
> And by this disobedient act
>   they sealed their mutual fate:
> The road to *Knowledge*
>   is the road that also leads to hell.
>
> When Moses led the Hebrews
>   out of Egypt's land, to find
> That other land the Chosen Ones
>   had long since left behind,
> With the serpent driven from his tree
>   – that old snake in the grass,
> The Father Figure who once ruled mankind
>   in Eden's Garden
> Lived in a box and wrought revenge,
>   bereft of love or pardon.
> Alas! But Moses bore aloft
>   a serpent made of brass.
>
> What had we wrought, how could it be,
>   that we had sunk so low?
> Our truly human souls had gone,
>   with further still to go;
> The spirit of mankind had reached
>   the level of the beast.
> For beasts rule by ferocity
>   and strength of tooth and claw,
> And Moses ruled by cruelty
>   and all-embracing LAW.
> He could not know it,
>   but it was the *serpent* he appeased.

And so down time we slid and slid,
   as though caught in a trance
Until we reached the spiritual stage
   of parity with plants;
And this for intellectual folk
   was quite beyond their ken.
The serpent ceased to rule the world
   and so (in Greece) did Pan,
And the ruler of the world
   became the quaintly named Green Man:
The symbol of the world of plants,
   of forest, bush and fen.

Now plants can seem quite docile things,
   quietly sitting still,
But if they can crush another plant,
   you can be sure they will:
Their life's a battlefield
   where victory is all and everything.
An ancient forest, we observe,
   is quite a peaceful place,
But once a gap appears,
   or falling trees create a space,
Each plant must fight to reach the sun,
   and each plant must be king!

When people's souls are filled by plants
   all striving for the kill,
Those people aim to overcome
   and bend folks to their will,
Though they can be very patient
   when o'ershadowed and suppressed.
Crusades and Jihads are the rule
   when Green Man has his say,
And lop and top and slash and burn
   are orders of the day.
Some may be still around right now
   — just put it to the test.

Ruled by the cruel laws of plants
        within the Green Man's sway,
A thousand years or two, we thought,
        is long enough to stay.
Materiality threatens now,
        men's souls to overwhelm.
Below the realm of plants are rocks
        and all that rocks contain
Like coal and oil and diamonds
        and every worldly gain:
Feared over past millennia
        as the dread Satanic realm!

His name is feared by pious men
        – a name with which to juggle,
A name associated with
        the great RELIGIOUS struggle:
Yes, it is he, the evil one,
        the tempter, or the devil.
Yet read it in the *Book of Job*
        (the eighteenth in the Bible)
That Satan is a son of God,
        to whom the Earth is liable.
He holds our souls in custody
        when we have reached his level.

So these four passions of the soul
        can hold men in their thrall,
They anchor us to Earth
        and keep us captives overall;
And none of them seen on its own
        is better than the rest.
But passions can be positive,
        if we seek this transition:
Faith rises from desire or greed,
        and from faith comes submission,
Submission subdues arrogance
        there lies the acid test.

The Human passion likes to learn,
        and practice observation,
The Serpent's passion is: coerce,
        and build a larger nation;
Without a firm foundation,
        both will wander aimlessly.
The Green Man has the passion
        of defensiveness and strife,
Under Satan's rule the passion is
        to live a wealthy life;
Harm only comes about
        when either rules exclusively.

So bear in mind that *balance* is essential
        for the soul
That wants to rise to heaven,
        its Creator to extol.
The passions cannot be denied,
        theirs is an iron rod.
But when these four flow equally
        in truly balanced fashion
They form the basis of a fifth:
        love, goodwill, or *compassion.*
That LOVE, you will discover,
        is the only way to God.

So be it told, and be it known,
        whatever your religion,
With love attained the soul can rise,
        completing Jacob's vision.
So best not leave your soul to fate,
        or nemesis, or karma;
Let passions cease, or stand aside,
        along with mind and heart.
Receive the contact with your soul,
        and let your journey start
Along that path that has been called
        Susila Budhi Dharma.

The Long Path of Purification

The instinctive route to regain Eden follows the slow path of purification. But, original human instinct having been set aside, by the way of the majority there is no through road. The higher worlds above cannot be reached. Those who stay as they are, remain as they are. Those who attain the limit of the occult path find themselves bathed in archangelic light, and of course wisdom or deep understanding is not the prerogative of people interested in the occult. They may not realise it, but the most brilliant scientists too "receive" their discoveries within this strange realm. The origins of the universe, remote space and beyond, all this is *material* knowledge. Clever people may discover real wisdom, but in spiritual terms its value is questionable. At the highest (and simultaneously the lowest) point of the satanic region, symbolically, are to be found the temple of Solomon and the gateway to *nirvana*. But even there the light is not the brilliant light of Spirit that "will appear and surround you".

This satanic realm is the home of wealth and wisdom, to be sure; the haunt of "spirit guides" and magicians; but the fearful "hot hells" of religious imagery are also there. For those of us who are not Solomon, or the Buddha, the light of Lucifer remains only the "pure white light" that at best can lead to a temporary heaven or paradise of the senses. Such a paradise will still be trapped within the web of *samsara*, still within materiality. Holy Spirit is the only guide that will set one's feet on the right path. Spirit is still the vehicle that can carry one's self beyond this web of becoming, and it is Spirit that, through us, can bring fresh vitality to the earth. In the original Hindu tradition:

The relentless current of time bears away all its results; even the good works done on earth come to an end and are gone forever. Those who do not find their soul in this world will not find their soul in any other. Those who do not find Spirit in this world will not find Spirit in any other.

Development of a True Culture

For those who *do* find Spirit in this world, the results as many can now attest are not all inward and abstract. One's "true talents" appear and become developed spontaneously to a personally astonishing degree – a "true culture" not connected with the superficial world of artifice and sophistry. Such a person will come to know instinctively what to do with plants, or with animals, and with people too – with regard perhaps to childbirth and infant care, should this become necessary. Deliberate desiring is not involved in this. Consciously to desire results one way or another simply cannot work for you in the way it once did, because "desiring" puts you back on the same footing as everyone else, but without the backing of materiality. In one sense, you will indeed be "less" than everyone else, because in some measure you will have lost the cooperation of Satan. It is an inward process manifesting in practical ways. It is not magic – indeed, quite the opposite. It is not science. It is not religion. It is not the province of *Sahid Anwas* or even of *Sahid Anwar*, but a recommencement of the original process of "dominion" over earth's creatures; a step towards the restoration of Eden.

4. STILLING THE PASSIONS

The Misleading Light of Lucifer

It should be plain enough by now, why it is said that the "true path" is narrow and somewhat precarious. We cannot shed our worldly "passions", we need to keep them all; and yet it is those same passions that normally preclude our meeting with Spirit and the means of gaining entry to the path. It has always been assumed by seers and mystics in the past that the passions must be denied if spiritual results are to be achieved. But I hope I have demonstrated that the outward-facing westward route following the strength of intellect is aimed at the wrong side of the mandala of life: it is aimed towards sunset, and the misleading light of Lucifer.

We return once again to the conflicting approaches of *Anwas* and *Anwar*, and now they seem more entangled than ever. The Buddhist aim is said to be *nirvana* – final extinction of the passions, though simple observation shows that *nirvana* was never really the goal of ordinary lay Buddhists. To them, also, it sounds too much like the final extinction of life. In any case, the global *nirvana* concept of a rotund world-Buddha bursting with rude health and haloed with the *aurora borealis*, represents an opting-out of the human race. We do not want nature to die, even if world-death carries with it the implication of rebirth in an improved condition. As for individual *nirvana*, it would seem to practical folk an unfortunate place to be: a condition of intellectual and emotional paralysis. The vibrations of life along with the passions, the pendulum of karma itself, would all have been stilled, and with them the expansive potential of Spirit, the possibilities both of *dhyana* and *dharma*. In a world context, it seems rather akin to doing nothing and allowing the worst to happen, allowing the earth to become a dead planet.

To *Sahid Anwar*, certainly, the cessation of physical desires and the extinction of emotional passions can only have a negative quality, if it lacks the uplifting grace of Spirit. For him, it implies death without redemption. If the ultimate attainment of *Anwas* is desired and motivated by those very passions of earthly will, such a destiny can only be contained within and limited by those controlling passions. To attain *nirvana*, in such a case, could involve only a further descent – albeit an incense-wafted descent – into some dank, airless oubliette beneath the spiritual household of mankind. To the Buddhist philosopher it is plain that the personal self does not correspond with spiritual reality. It has to be set aside; but this unreal self is itself compounded of the passions which rule life. The endless cycling of death and rebirth, operative from one level of understanding to the next, will, he knows, continue only whilst he still identifies with that unstable ego.

A Personal Family of Souls

To understand a principle, however, and actually to put the workings of it into practice, are two different things. It cannot really be done "by oneself". The transition from an attitude of *Anwas* to one of *Anwar*, then, is an essential requirement, and perhaps a significant step in this transition is a growing understanding that "self is not yet", that what we have in the here and now, is "soul". But this understanding is quickly complicated by the discovery that there is more than one soul, more than one *sukma*, any of which may hold sway in the world of *samsara*, the world of *nafsu*. They may come into conscious awareness, but only contact with Spirit and the gradual formation of *Jiwa* will bring these lower souls, these "brothers" who constitute the human family, into productive unity.

To identify these souls we need to look again at the life forces which control the world of *samsara*, for the two principles correspond by nature, and together form the basis of man's life on earth, both material and spiritual. Depending upon which life force is currently to the fore as the leading passion, forming as it were a centre of gravity within the individual, a soul, or one aspect of the soul, can be understood to have acquired a selection of characteristics from these instinctual forces, blending with personal contents, and giving it an individual identity. These characteristics, once established and united as a soul in its own right, and sharing to some extent the nature of material objects, of plants, or animals, or ordinary humans, may accurately be termed "driving passions". To the *rochani* eyes of one who has made the ascent, and sometimes to the sensitive *raewani* eyes of one who has been inspired but not yet begun to climb, these souls or occupying passions are actually to be seen as subtle versions of the individual, filled, motivated, and coloured by the lower life force of which they are representative.

The Coloured Brothers of Passion

The so-called "black" passion corresponds with the material forces as they operate within the selfhood of man. A "black magician" was – or indeed still is, though seldom correctly identified as such – one who has developed this material passion in himself to a supernatural degree. The chief characteristic of "black brother" is greed, involving the gathering of benefits to oneself. These benefits may have the appearance of unselfishness, involving family, livelihood, or nationality. It is this black passion that has the ability to manipulate solid matter, to acquire and confer the wealth and wisdom of Solomon. Satan is truly the god of cleverness!

Other passions or souls are of a higher, more refined and therefore perhaps more truly spiritual nature than the material, but they cannot by themselves acquire or confer either treasure or wisdom. In the world of the *Asuras*, the fierce plant passions by themselves, though firmly rooted to satanic earth, have no knowledge or wisdom beyond their own need for survival, for reproduction, for strife, for ruthlessness. Neither can the animals through their passions, free to roam the earth yet lacking the power of reason, acquire material benefits beyond their basic instinctive needs.

Understandably the black passion has been dubbed "the tempter", "the deceiver", or "the adversary", because its magnetic attraction, so hard to resist, virtually constitutes a gravitational pull away from spirituality, away from the divine source. Denied to plants and animals, as a part of mankind through which the vibration of materiality – the satanic force – can operate, "black brother" can be a source of guidance to knowledge, possessions, self-preservation and worldly influence.

The "red" passion corresponds with the plant life forces, and the chief characteristic of red brother is arrogant competitiveness, with violent activity punctuated by spells of indolence. When considered as an individual, he is not greatly tied to family or social circle, and though this "soul" provides much of the motivation, the thrust and constructive energy behind successful business, being "rooted to the earth" it relies heavily upon information provided by its black brother, the satanic passion. The ancient Tibetan Buddhists described a glowing red light as representative of the environment most attractive to plants, and to those humans who have plant essence as their centre of gravity. In horticultural terms, an environment bathed in infra-red light is a luxuriant paradise for plants.

It is the "yellow" passion that corresponds with the instinctual forces of animal life, and its chief characteristic is desire. It is not concerned with long-term ambitions so much as short-term gains, and these are usually connected with food or sex. Individuals dominated by the yellow soul, however, usually follow a conventional, well modulated lifestyle, as indeed do animals in nature. Being free individually to a much greater degree than any plant, animals are reasonably adaptable and comparatively unselfish. The family unit is important to most animals, and the same applies to a human being who is dominated by his own "yellow brother".

The "white" passion corresponds with the human life forces. An individual who has "white brother" as his centre of gravity will be greatly concerned with observing, understanding, and analysing the world around him. But he may well seem oddly naive or childlike when his understanding is not counterbalanced by the direct, practical approach of the material black passion.

To *Anwas* eyes an element of blueness appears in the higher regions of these passions. The human passion which I have described as white may be seen as pale blue, whilst the animal passion, being yellow now tinged with blue, will be seen as green. This accords with the "colours of the places of rebirth" described in the *Tibetan Book of the Dead*. On an ancient prayer mat from Muttra, an early Indian centre of the "new" religion of Buddhism, the Buddha was depicted as brown – the amalgam of all passions – and the smaller bodhisattvas surrounding him displayed the colours of the separate passions, the separate "souls" of those who have not yet attained buddhahood: Black, red, yellow (or green) and white (or blue). This is an important point, this "brownness" of the Buddha. It has frequently been the aim of *Anwas* seekers to attempt to regain the truly human level. But if they were to succeed, by lacking the lower attributes typified by the "brothers", they would be weak and helpless, unable to make tools or weapons, unable even to defend themselves against the rigours of nature. Buddhahood implies an even balance of all these passions, an amalgamation of souls to produce a new soul which we call "brown brother".

Aiming For the Truly Human Level

The ideal aim of both *Anwar* and *Anwas*, by rejecting the lower influences by whatever name they may have been known, has been to regain the truly human level as distinct from the "ordinary human level" of white brother. It may be called the "saintly level", not because those people who in the past have been declared saints, had necessarily arrived at that spiritual level, but because the name *rochani* which describes it implies that such a person has gained the level of spiritual love – which characterised such as Jesus himself. Many seekers of the *Anwas* type, in particular Hindus and Buddhists, have tried to help the process along by abandoning their material possessions, home and family. Many sincere seekers in the

the sage Yajnavalkya to Janaka, king of Videha: *"I have found the narrow path known of old, that stretches far away. By this path the sages who know the Spirit ascend to the regions of heaven and thence to liberation. The path is adorned with white and blue, yellow and green and red. This is the path of the seers of Brahman"*. But even A*tman* and *Brahman*, expressing spiritual possibilities in personal terms, seem to change in their definition page by page. Reassembled in the light of *Susila Budhi Dharma*, the message of these verses is pure and simple. Running backwards in time, their conclusion is also their source, the source of *dhyana*, and the source of all life.

A Summary of the Spiritual Journey

It makes sense to begin with one highly significant verse which we now see as the key that, for people of all religions or none, will unlock the door and open the path to life:

True teachers are not those well versed in sacred books. True teachers are those who have contact with eternity through Spirit. To the pupil who approaches a true teacher with mind, heart and senses at peace, is opened the way to Spirit.

Clever men hold that the chemistry of nature brings about life, the birth of men and planets. Others speak of abstract time and the permutations of chance. But wise men see that the glory of God alone brings about the cycle of life, both elemental and complex.

God may be seen by the pure in heart; so say the sages. But where is a heart that is pure? Faith in the God of love is a saving grace; faith in the love of God can lift one to grace, leaving behind the endless succession of birth and death.

Every man is his own judge. All his past actions are reflected on him alone at death. All his deeds, thoughts and desires are stored within his own soul.

The human soul may be light and airy, or heavy and earthly, according to the weight of past thoughts and actions. Thoughts and actions can lead on to freedom, or hold in thraldom through life after life, through death after death.

Those who follow action alone fall into deep darkness. Those who follow knowledge alone fall into even deeper darkness. There are worlds of darkness awaiting those who ignore the light.

Even the humblest mind can learn this great truth: there are not many, but only one. He who sees only variety where there is unity is obliged to wander aimlessly from death to death. All things work together for the good.

He who sees only the variety and not the unity, is doomed to wander on from death to death. This is the fate of the beasts. Even by the earthly mind this truth must be seen: There are not many, but only one.

God has given man power over the beasts. By the interflow of souls, power exercised without tranquillity draws a man downwards. His children become unwilling recipients of his brutality; they bear the fruits of his passions.

The man who lives in desire goes to birth and death again, according to the pattern of his desiring. Myths tell of birth and death vying for power, but simple acceptance is greater than either.

The flame of life springs from something greater than itself. Wise men in their meditation surrender their flame to that which is greater. By allowing their thoughts, their passions, and their senses to subside and be still, they attain the Spirit that gives eternal life.

There are two ways to receive that which is from Spirit: in silence, and in sound. Neither are from man's volition, for by Spirit volition is withdrawn, and by volition Spirit is withdrawn. Preoccupied silence, by employing volition, precludes Spirit. Spiritual silence is the stilling of passions, and the peace of eternity.

In meditation from man's volition there is speech and silence, movement and rest. In meditation from Spirit there is speech and silence, movement and rest − without man's volition. Speech and movement animate the physical body, but the mover is Spirit.

138

The peace of contemplation may be sought in beautiful places, free from pollution, smoke, noise and foul smells. But Spirit has no preference for places. Spirit may dwell in the soul of man amidst noise and bustle and confusion, for the peace of God is within, embracing all.

In life and in nature the body of man lacks pure consciousness. Who has the power to will consciousness to his own body? But there is a place in man where Spirit may enter, unbeknown. Within that place supreme consciousness grows and radiates.

Consciousness should be the goal of all men. Dreamers dream that they have it already; thinkers think that they have it already; boasters boast that they have it already.

When consciousness governs speech, we speak to all men. When consciousness governs breath, we breathe unsuspected perfumes. When consciousness governs sight, we see immaterial forms. When consciousness governs hearing, we hear unuttered words. When consciousness governs thinking, we know the unknowable.

Knowledge of the soul is reached through sincerity and truth. Knowledge of Spirit is reached through the grace of God. Knowledge of God is reached through the purifying force of Spirit.

The fabric of man's feelings is woven through and through with threads of error and sin – the results of wrong thoughts, pride, and harmful behaviour. The soul of man, with his will, his mind and his heart, is powerless to remove these alien threads. Spirit alone has the cleansing power.

Though the sun shines on pleasure and suffering alike, it is untouched and unaffected by earthly passions. So the Spirit, both inside and out, is untouched and unaffected by earthly passions.

Man's body is a castle with eleven gates; so said the ancients. When Spirit dwells in the soul of man, man's body is known as a glorious temple. The mortal body remains under the power of pain and death; but the soul can rise to Supreme Spirit, and find there its glorious body of light.

Soul of man is the consciousness of life, the witness of all actions, and the light of the heart. Soul contains all the contents of man. Spirit entering the soul of man is joined with mortal sin; but when Spirit wills, he cleans the temple and ejects evil.

When the soul is brought to the awareness of Spirit, an inner gate is opened. With silence and with shouts, with joy and with suffering, the alien threads of sin are withdrawn.

Wise men speak of higher soul, and lower soul – and they speak the truth. Lower soul is the soul of man alone, bound by the gross elements – by the passions of good and bad, light and dark. Higher soul is Spirit in the soul of man.

Higher soul, whose content is Spirit, is immortal, free from light and darkness, reward and punishment which influence human thoughts and actions; free from rebirth, pride, desire, and death. Lower soul, whose content is the inner feeling of man, falls oft into confusion, finding itself swept helplessly along in the turbid waters of earthly life.

When man entertains thoughts of self, or pride, or of desire, he binds himself wholly to his lower soul, careless of Spirit and ignorant of the will of God. His passage through life is confused and uncertain, wandering blindly along false paths.

The soul may be understood by a subtle mind in the silence of meditation. But Spirit cannot be understood.

By the grace of wisdom and sincerity, the soul may be seen in the silence of meditation. But Spirit cannot be envisaged.

Spirit cannot be seen by mortal eye. Spirit cannot be approached by mortal mind or senses. Words cannot reveal him, but when he takes his throne he makes his presence known.

The human soul is called the son of man, inheritor of all that man is and does. Spirit in the soul of man is called the son of God, inheritor of all that God is and does, lord of mankind.

Only those who see the radiance of Spirit within their own souls can hope to see the universal radiance of God's dwelling.

140

Only those who know the guidance of Spirit in this world can hope to receive the guidance of Spirit in worlds to come.

In wonder and in silence the wise man acknowledges Spirit as the eternal guide for all creation. Thenceforth, all his works will be holy works, whether great or small. In domestic affairs and in the affairs of nations, all his works will be holy works, whether great or small. In Spirit alone he seeks peace and joy.

Nature is created for the sake of soul – the means whereby to feel, to taste, to explore, to grow away, and to return with wisdom renewed. Mankind is fated to grow away from the love of God in order to return with wisdom renewed.

Pure consciousness within all conscious beings, God alone is eternal amongst things that pass away. Only Spirit can carry man's awareness into the realms of God.

Dwelling beyond the range of human eyesight, God can be neither seen nor understood. But when Spirit enters the soul of man, his heart and mind are filled with the knowledge of God.

Between the vibrations of light, beyond the darkness of space, is a glorious region of splendour from whence came all light. Only God with his Spirit is there.

God with his Spirit is pure consciousness, the creator of time. God is all powerful and all knowing, the creator of space, suns and whirling planets. Under his rule are the elements and the evolution of life.

God with his Spirit is hidden in all things, at the innermost soul of all beings. Beyond the laws and conditions of nature, beyond the understanding of man, he watches over all the works of his creation, great and small.

Those who see Spirit in this life become free from the cycle of nature. Those who find their own souls as a little child filled with Spirit, become free from the cycle of birth and death.

What may seem at first a taste of sweetness may become a vile cup of poison. What may seem at first a cup of sorrow may become a glorious draught of immortality. The path of wisdom may lead through pain and grief to the end of all suffering.

In this world people have much cleverness but little wisdom. In the innermost being of those whose unwisdom is changed by Spirit, their developing wisdom becomes a beacon for their journey. They see the way to God illumined by their own inner radiance.

Spirit is beyond fate. He watches over the lives of men, experiences everything, and bestows his blessings where he will. Who recognises Spirit and understands the ever changing conditions of nature is no longer propelled towards death.

Spirit dwells in the soul of man, but the foolish see only the man. All their earthly hopes are ill founded, their learning in vain. They are destined to sink into a world of demons; to sink deeper into the darkness of delusion.

Even the humblest or most sinful of people who seek shelter of Spirit attain the supreme path. To love Spirit with sincerity, with all one's soul, brings soul and Spirit together in harmony.

It is a promise of Spirit: "Whosoever loves me shall not perish". Even the wickedest of men must be considered righteous, if he accepts Spirit with sincerity.

The soul of man enjoys the bodily senses of the moment as a bee sips the nectar of beautiful flowers. With Spirit, becoming free from the cycle of nature, he becomes the lord of all time, past, present and future.

When childish innocence is lost, Spirit is forgotten. But when knowledge of Spirit is regained, childish innocence returns to the soul. In truth, man becomes again as a little child.

Spirit appears in the soul of man when the senses are stilled, as in a sleeping child; when the powers of life are all one. Though men may say: "The breath of life is gone", soul and Spirit are one in eternity.

When all the bonds that tie the soul to the heart are loosened, when all the desires that cling to the heart are abandoned, mortal man becomes immortal; material man becomes immaterial, evermore one with Spirit.

Even with great knowledge, Spirit cannot be reached until the senses are at rest, until the mind and the passions are at peace. Spirit is reached by those of his choosing, because they accept him on his own terms.

To those whom Spirit chooses he reveals his glory. A man may long for Spirit; a man may think he chooses Spirit; but Spirit is not to be gained by wishing or choosing; Spirit chooses.

When a man knows Spirit he is free. His doubts are at an end, and the cycle of birth and death is no more. Transcending the world of the body through inner union, he finds the world of Spirit in which he is one with God.

Those who have experienced truth can be the teachers of truth. Those who have experienced Spirit can be the teachers of Spirit. Ask from them to be taught; their knowledge is pure wisdom.

There are many seemingly endless paths of men, but all in the end must come to Spirit. In whatever way a man finds to love Spirit, in that way will Spirit accept him; in that way will he find spiritual love.

Spirit is one and the same to all beings — to people of all religions and races. Those who with sincerity worship Spirit, dwell in Spirit, and Spirit dwells in them.

All worlds pass away, only to return in a never ending cycle; but whoever goes to Spirit, stays with Spirit, and journeys no more from death to death.

All things pass away, but Spirit will not pass away. Spirit has dominion over all things, and the wise who recognise him in their own souls can find eternal peace.

When Spirit enters in, the soul of man knows fulfilment. Though pangs and sorrows may still come through past misdeeds, all suffering is made bearable through the joy of Spirit.

When Spirit in the soul of man is known and witnessed, ancient fears that assailed the heart are relieved; ancient doubts that clouded the mind blow away, and the restless pendulum of karma sways softly to a standstill.

143

Spirit in the soul of man – inner light of the inner self – encompasses the whole of life: Awareness, reason, thought; the passions of man; the actions of seeing, speaking, hearing, touching, smelling, tasting; all things find their peace in Spirit.

When salt is added to water it cannot be seen, yet it fills the water and can be tasted on every side. So is Spirit in the soul of man. It cannot be seen, but its presence is known, and it affects the awareness of all who are touched.

In truth, Spirit is not to be sought in vanity; neither is Spirit to be sought in seeking; neither is Spirit to be sought in desire; neither is Spirit to be sought in abstinence; neither is Spirit to be sought in a life of wandering.

Spirit is not to be attained by will. Will sets man apart from Spirit. Exercise of the will sets up an impenetrable shield, hiding the light of Spirit.

Spirit within the soul of man requires the obedience of love and truth; they are the property of Spirit. Those who by finding their own soul receive Spirit in this world, inherit the freedom of Spirit in worlds to come. They possess the seed of immortality.

Spirit is the beginning and the end of all life; the secret behind the mystery of birth and death.

Spirit is beyond earthly life, yet shares in it. Never born and never to die, he watches over the life and death and deeds of men, dwelling secretly in the soul, eternal messenger and guide to the infinite source of all creation.

Spirit is the key to eternity, eternal messenger of God, guiding the steps of man through the terrors of death.

God is beyond sound and form, above all reasoning, without caste or creed or religion, without touch or taste or smell. God is eternal and unchangeable, without beginning or end. When consciousness of God is brought to the soul of man by Spirit, that man becomes freed from death.

To approach God is to overcome death; his is the only path that leads to eternal life. Spirit brings the fire of hope to the deep ocean, guiding us through life by his light. His radiance illumines all creation; when a man approaches God through Spirit, he is freed from all his bonds.

The grace of God moves our souls and bodies without our volition. Through his quickening Spirit he leads us into his own joy, and into the glory of his universal light.

God is unknown to those who think he can be known by thought. God is unknown to the learned man, and known to the newborn child.

Knowledge of God cannot be taught by those who have not reached him. God cannot be reached by high thoughts; he is higher than the highest thoughts. He is not to be attained by reasoning.

God is farther away than the farthest star. God is nearer than the breath we breathe. God is closer to us than our own selves. God is everywhere.

When the wise man senses the full glory of God, Spirit, Creator, he leaves multiplicity behind with the folly of desire, and goes forward to unity.

When the passions of man flow together in Spirit, they create love. Where there is no love, there is no Spirit.

Love is not a choice to be made; love is a state to be attained. Those who attain it are five times blessed.

Love was first-born in creation, existing before the world of men. Love goes where Spirit goes, and Spirit goes everywhere.

Love is a condition of God, a quality of Spirit, a key to the path. Without love, the final barrier will never be raised. Love is a coming together of the family of man, both within and beyond his earthly temple.

Messengers of God and the Great Life Force

This is the simple foundation on which all subsequent complications have been built. The reality and the symbol can now be differentiated for good. One feels intuitively that the message re-emerging, the means to return to the source which is at the base of all religions, is the same in essence as the direct receiving of the messengers of God in past ages – Jesus Christ, the Prophet Mohammad, Sheikh Abd al-Qadr al-Jailani, and, of more relevance to us today, Muhammad Subuh Sumohadiwidjojo who also received this Great Life Force, accompanied this time by his own particular brand of exegesis – the unwilled ability to pass on the practical proof of this receiving to others on request, to channel the reality of this, the essence of all religions, to all future generations.

As *Atman*, the *sukma* – the collective but also the individual lower soul in man – is the point at which *nafsu* and *Jiwa* meet; where the material influences of the world can be pierced by Spirit. By itself, *sukma* could well be called the Babylon of the inner self, the 'Gateway to God' able to be used by influences high and low. As *Brahman*, as *Jiwa*, as Spirit within the soul of man, *sukma* becomes a temple within the material self, able to contain that which is spiritual – a place by which it is possible to receive guidance directly from the power of Almighty God. This is *Aras Allah*, the seat of God in man, the centre of consciousness in the young child, the centre of consciousness of the saint, and it is indeed the source from which the answers to all the world's problems are to be found. This is the *sukma* who, with the help of *Jiwa*, can analyse soil in a trice and inform the farmer of the deficiency; who can scan a whole library of books in an instant, and indicate the volume, page and paragraph required; the source not only of lowly *dhyana*, but of divine wisdom too. But this fount of knowledge can only be accepted with truly humble sincerity. It is not meant as a brain-booster; it is a brain modifier, and it was never needed more than now. In this, the reality of the spiritual path is indeed a great blessing; but the earth itself is still in jeopardy.

A Centre of Consciousness

It was no mere ignorant vanity that led early religionists to the concept that the world lay at the centre of the universe, and that Jerusalem – or whatever spot may have been taken to represent the holiest place – was sited at the centre of the world. Different world

146

religions have represented the spiritual aspect of mankind in various ways, but always the human centre of gravity has been visualised exactly at the halfway point in the scale of life forces that fill the universe, midway between the lowest material life force, *roh sjetaniah,* the realm of Satan, and the highest, *roh rabbaniah,* the abode of God.

Concern for the health and well-being of the planet is a material concern, which is not to say a "non-spiritual" concern. Materiality in the spiritual scale, as we apprehend it, although so far inferior to the "truly human" level of being, actually constitutes the spiritual centre of gravity of the human race as it is, apart from a comparative handful of individuals. So if it is really true that the world's problems are actually spiritual rather than material problems — material impoverishment on the spiritual plane — it follows that it cannot be feasible to expect human beings, no matter how individually clever, to manage or modify the world in such a way as to heal its ills.

A World Teacher to Start a Chain Reaction

As Gurdjieff might have put it, none but a "man No. 7" could command the satanic forces of materiality effectively enough really to control them. A man No.6 may be able to control them to a fair extent, a man No.5 to a very small extent, and men Nos.4, 3, 2 and 1, not at all. A powerful man No.1 will certainly *think* that he can control the forces of materiality, but is liable to discover at the end of his life that, all along, *they* have been controlling *him.* A man No.2, like the plants, can do no more than modify the surface or the surface covering of materiality. A man No.3, like the animals, can do little more than scratch a hole for himself to sit in, and maintain the *status quo.* But "if you want to change the world, first change yourself". Once a man No.7 has sparked off the chain reaction, men Nos.1, 2, and 3, if they aspire to do so, can gradually become men Nos.4, 5 and 6. When enough people above the fifth *rochani* level of spiritual development become deeply enough aware of a worldwide problem, conditions should automatically change very rapidly for the better, through a surge of natural growth originating from within.

Gurdjieff fully expected a real man No.7 to arrive on the scene, and so he did. Pak Subuh was probably unique among 20th century men in being able to give truly spiritual advice from firsthand experience. But he had far more than that to give. As I write, several thousand people have been able to endorse the reality of that old Hindu verse: "True teachers are those who have contact with eternity through Spirit. To the pupil who approaches such a teacher with mind, heart and senses at peace, is opened the way to Spirit". Gurdjieff himself never lived to see the arrival in the west of the long-awaited World Teacher.

The Contact : Opening the Soul

A Muslim with the wonderfully pliable foundation of Javan Hindu culture, Pak Subuh told us how as a young man he had pursued a quest for spiritual knowledge, in common with others of his time and place. He found however that the gurus whom he approached could tell him nothing of value, only that he would later find out everything for himself. Discouraged, he abandoned his search for higher things and resigned himself to the humdrum routine of raising a family and earning a living. It was only then, after relinquishing his desire to seek God, that he was blessed with a series of strange experiences that brought him to the reality of *Susila Budhi Dharma*. From that time until his death in 1987 he was able to pass on the benefit of his receiving — a spiritual contact which is still available to all who sincerely want it, and who are prepared to accept such responsibilities as may arise in the process which follows it. The contact does nothing except lay the soul open by allowing the "passions" which have overlaid it during our lives, to be temporarily laid aside. The name *Subud*, as I mentioned before, is a contraction of the three Sanskrit words *Susila Budhi Dharma*, and has no more than a coincidental resemblance to Subuh, the name of its founder.

The *Subud* contact, known as the "opening", is brought about and subsequently reinforced by simple submission to higher powers, in the company of others who have already been "opened". No physical contact is involved. It is the only means, as far as I know, whereby the power of the material, the plant, and the animal life forces, the passions and worldly influences which always interfere and control the lives of men, can be temporarily set aside, opening the way for finer influences to be felt. The mind and the emotions remain fully awake and functional during the receiving, and are made keenly aware of all that transpires, but they do not take part. They are able merely to act as witnesses – an audience to the quickening of the soul through the ingress of Spirit, in an individual "direct receiving" from a source higher than one's own everyday self.

This receiving, and the physical movements that sooner or later arise spontaneously as a result, amount to a kind of spiritual exercise, and are known in *Subud* by the Indonesian word *latihan*. The will should not be in the least involved in these movements; there is no exercise to practice in the usual sense of the word; there are no rites to follow and no theories to learn or to pursue in *Subud*. It is a process not likely to be confused with any of the various methods of numbing consciousness or awakening inner awareness that were previously known to seekers after truth. It is simply a matter of putting aside heart and mind and allowing the unencumbered soul to express itself and grow.

Stillness holds the key –
The still small voice
that arises from the void
that lies between these two contenders:
vehement thoughts
and passionate feelings,
when they separate
and stand aside.

For divine truth comes not from trembling bodies
or violent actions
or tempestuous convictions
or penetrating thoughts
or burning desires
or all-consuming emotions,
but from the stillness that arises
when these false claimants are stilled.

Allowing the Newly Opened Soul to Exercise

When confronted with a totally new experience, a totally unfamiliar concept, it can be useful to use descriptive terms which are also new and unfamiliar. One might suppose that the term "spiritual exercise" could be used in English speaking countries rather than the Indonesian equivalent: *latihan kejiwaan*. Why not use plain English? Some people have expressed a wish to describe the *latihan* and matters of the *kejiwaan* by using modern psychological terminology. But it is in our common nature to hang labels onto unfamiliar things and by so doing, to imagine that we already understand them. We each have our own preconception of "exercise" and our own idea of "spiritual": put the two together and we are likely to think; "Oh, that!" It is *not* a good idea to imagine that we already understand the *latihan,* or that it is something familiar.

In simplistic terms, the *latihan* is a short period of time set aside for the express purpose of allowing the soul to exercise without the interference of mind and heart, without either deliberate action or inaction. Those who happen to be acquainted with charismatic religious movements, or with "speaking in tongues", will doubtless assume that they already possess the *latihan.* Self-analysts accustomed to focusing their attention on the backcloth of consciousness may be convinced that they already know it. Yogis and monks, faith healers, trance-practitioners, present-day witches, warlocks and magicians, will all almost certainly consider themselves experts before the event. People who have experimented with mind-altering drugs, and psychiatric specialists in the unconscious mind, may feel that this "spiritual exercise" involves the exploration of territory already familiar to them. But, in truth, as *Subud* people are in a position to assert, the *latihan kejiwaan* is not "just this" or "just that" — it embraces all and everything. *Subud* embraces all things and all experiences, as indeed Almighty God by definition must encompass all things, good and bad, high and low.

It is the *latihan* state of awareness that represents a return to Eden in practice, recalling a time in man's prehistory when thoughts and feelings had not yet become all-demanding, when Adam and Eve were prompted to action not by will but by Spirit. This state has been compared with the *Qadr* described by the Prophet Mohammed, whilst references to "receiving the Holy Spirit" within the Christian tradition also seem open to this interpretation. But *Subud* is not a religion, and the advice of its founder is that it should never be thought of in this way. It is available equally to followers of different religions, and to those many who follow no organised religious system at all.

Subud is Not a Teaching

Pak Subuh gave numerous explanations from his experience concerning the field of the *kejiwaan*, and frequently gave advice to *Subud* members, whether asked or not. But he has never passed on any kind of teaching to be followed, nor has he issued directives to be obeyed. The distinguishing feature of the freedom that lies beyond religions, beyond Zen, and beyond philosophical systems of self-help, is that no man can claim to stand between the individual and the power of God, between man and his maker. One comes to discover the practical truth that lies behind all religions, for all the great religions are true in their own way, if they can be understood correctly. By following the *latihan kejiwaan* of *Subud* one's own religion, or religious attitude and its spiritual content, can eventually be clearly understood — in Islam, for instance, by bringing about the reality and freedom of the *hakekah* as opposed to the binding obligations of the *sharia*.

151

But religions as such have been created, or have become over time an agency, for the comfort and guidance of the heart rather than the soul. On the path of *Susila Budhi Dharma* there are no arbitrary laws to be obeyed; the one giving instructions, delegated by the power of God, is Spirit working through *Jiwa*: the high soul, holy son and lord of mankind. All else, all other personal contents that the individual brings to the *latihan*, are automatically set aside and become quiescent. To follow the *latihan* of *Subud* and the movement of the *Jiwa*, therefore, is to follow the way of reality.

The Way of Reality

As an example of the relationship between religious observance and spiritual reality, if one is a Muslim, in the *hakekah* one's orientation is not towards a certain place or any particular direction, but "inwards" towards oneself, towards one's own inner nature, and thus simultaneously "outwards" towards God. The practicality of this is that anyone can be aware of God and of his own true self at any time and in any place. As the ancient wisdom had it: "It is wrong not to seek God, but it is also wrong to seek God, for God is already closer to man than his own imagining". Once the *hakekah* has been established, merely by quietening his thoughts and feelings a person can instantly be in touch with the life of the *Jiwa*, quite independently of time, place, environment, or compass point. Such a person's receiving is inward, where there is need neither for tangible symbols nor for religious reminders of one's place in the universe.

But while we live on earth, we are subject to the conditions of the earth. We are all to a great degree the slaves of our environment, and distressful circumstances of a practical nature do not make it any easier to receive grace. The strength of the *nafsu* is such that outward influences normally take precedence over inner peace, and bad conditions in the form of pain, hunger, poverty, hopelessness, and the inevitability of death, may tend to create a vicious circle of despair. It behoves those of us who *are* in a favourable situation of life, and who are not wholly preoccupied with merely staying alive, or searching for the next scrap of food, to take full advantage of their good fortune by seeking this contact with Spirit, and allowing the process to take place. To deny grace and good fortune for oneself out of distorted sympathy for others less fortunately placed, is not going to help their situation one jot. No one is going to envy you the *latihan kejiwaan* which cannot be seen or pictured, because it precipitates not an outward but an inward process.

The Soul as Helmsman of the Psyche

No doubt there have been numerous culturally variable concepts of some sort of vital urge centred in man's being. In psychological terms we may speak of *libido* which, if denied, can cause neurotic symptoms and social problems. If this driving seat of "wanting" is seen as *sukma*, ever-present though not "opened" to receive the power of Spirit, and not in conscious communication with the brain, it should give a fairly accurate picture of the overall effect that the contents of this, our lower soul, can have on our behaviour, and on our mental and emotional health. The soul is, or should be, the leader, the helmsman of the psyche. At the *Subud* opening, when the lower soul, *sukma,* is given a separate conscious existence powered, as it were, by the higher soul, *Jiwa,* we become able to see the hitherto unsuspected nature of its contents, and it also becomes easy for us to understand why for so long it has had so potent an influence on our actions and attitudes.

In the reality of the *hakekah*, the receiving of each one who takes part is uniquely personal, and the course of the *latihan kejiwaan*, in both the short and the long term, will be different for each. It is not a case of "pick and choose", as though there were an option between courses of instruction depending on the personality or psychological type of the individual. There can be no choice of receiving, for the receiving comes about only by the will of God, through the nature only of one's own true self. Indeed, when personal choice enters in, the process ceases to be a *latihan* of the *Jiwa*, and becomes merely an exercise of the heart.

Seduced by "Speaking in Tongues"

The process of spiritual purification can sometimes be a noisy business, and pride can grow insidiously with the miraculous utterance of unbidden words. It involves the disgorging of unwanted personal contents, often in the form of garbled words and sentences. Sometimes these words seem beautiful and meaningful, real "soul poetry". Sometimes they will be frankly unpleasant. It is best to treat them all as verbal vomit rather than something precious or holy. Some people are seduced by the utterances of their own *sukma*, enthusiastically adding their own preconceptions and quite wrongly taking it all to be something on a par with "the very word of God". At a much higher level than the majority can hope ever to experience, this throwing out of soul contents can indeed be truly inspired and of great benefit to others: the speech of the sage is also his purification. Bapak's talks and explanations were certainly of this nature. But for sage and simpleton alike, it is a slow and continual process. Those who speak naively of their own "purified soul", or who describe others seemingly less advanced than themselves as being "unpurified", are dangerously misled.

To a *Subud* person, *sukma* is quickly forgotten, and *Jiwa* becomes all-important. Nothing but the entry of Spirit into the personal lower soul can displace the impurities that have been building up within our souls since the time of our birth and even before that event, and it will be a gradual process. It is precisely this piecemeal removal of ingrained faults that produces the language of *dharma*, and the truly involuntary but wholly conscious phenomenon of "tongues". The process *has* to be involuntary to have value. The slightest hint of determination, the adoption of an attitude, a deliberate setting in motion, the odd throwing in of a phrase or two, any of this will check the progress of the *latihan*.

Understanding "*latihan* talk" is natural to some and alien to others, depending largely as it does on the function of introverted

154

heart – the emotions – follows soon after. The intellectual process remains "unplugged-in" for many years. Ideas are received without effort, and they may fall into place in matters of planning and design. But competitors with keener brains may still be able to outsmart you, and beat you in some material goal, some choice contract. The *latihan* is a *latihan kejiwaan*, and not a means of making money. There will always be exceptions. The amazing happy miracle can still occur when needed most, but it is never down to the brain, and it can never be forecast. We may conclude that it is better if your daily occupation has a strongly physical bias during these early years of *Jiwa* motivation. Where brains are concerned, the will is bound always to be paramount, and this type of will is the very quality that proves incompatible with *Jiwa*. The best laid schemes "gang aft a-gley" whether *Subud* is behind them or not.

When the time comes for a change of perception, a change of occupation, a change of skills, one will be left in no doubt as to the nature of helplessness, for any or all these *Jiwa*-led skills and energies may instantly disappear. One's machines will no longer run as they should. One's tool-hand will no longer be unerring. One's energy will no longer be focused as before. One must move on. One will be compelled to take up new skills and adopt new aims, for beneath and behind all these experiences it is the whole individual self that must develop and progress, rather than a small patch of the material world and its problems. Nothing can stand still for long without stagnation.

Subud is Ourselves

It is important to realise that *Susila Budhi Dharma*, that *Subud*, is neither a "way" nor a religion, in the normally understood meanings of these words. Nor is it something that has to be followed or believed in or obeyed. It is not a method or style of living, not some fount of inspiration for the brain, nor even a mark of spirituality. The exercise which we call the *latihan kejiwaan*, and all these mystical communal experiences which I have hinted at are not the aim or the outcome of *Subud*. All these are mere stages in the coming to awareness of soul. *Subud* includes every state and every possibility within itself, because *Subud* is ourselves: our developing selves with all our own contents and possibilities. The only worldly outcome of *Subud*, therefore, is the normal, everyday life and the changing perceptions of the people involved.

5. The World Unified

The Nature of Subud

Susila Budhi Dharma is a state, a sought-after condition of life, the actuality of all religious aspiration. *Subud*, on the other hand, is merely an organisation. So is it possible, many have wondered, to study *Subud*, to understand its methods, sample its "technique", imbibe its content, as if it were another website to be studied, or book to be read, or guru to be visited?

To do this, to take *Subud* as a religious movement or a philosophical system, is to reduce the reality of *Susila Budhi Dharma* to its mere concept – the ritual without the content, the *sharia* without the *hakekah,* the form without the Spirit. It is also to court disappointment. *Subud* cannot be merely an organisation apart from the people who have been opened and who take part in it. *Subud is* people, and the desire to *be Subud* must be submissive and come from within.

Let me relate a personal experience which may illustrate in practical terms what Subud is all about: When Pak Subuh visited London in the early spring of 1967 I went to one of the Subud gatherings which was held in a large meeting hall. Characteristic of those comparatively early Subud gatherings, several hundred Subud members were present, not just from Britain but from all over the world. I arrived rather late, just before the latihan was about to commence. I had been opened in Subud only since the previous year, and I still felt somewhat awkward and unworthy, very conscious of all my faults and weaknesses – very much the odd one out. Bapak glanced at me as I came in, and I remember thinking: "What am I doing in this sort of company? I'm not wanted here. Well, if you don't want me, Bapak, I'll be off!" The latihan commenced, and all those hundreds of people began their whirling and wailing, singing, crying, laughing, running and dancing. I still stood near the door. Bapak was somewhere on the other side of that huge room, and in between us that swirling mass of bodies. Suddenly, a broad, clear corridor of empty space opened between us as the crowd of people parted, as if swept to either side, each individual immersed in his own latihan and, of course, quite oblivious to my own little drama. As we stood, Bapak and I, looking at each other from either end of this broad strip of empty carpet, I felt the most indescribable wave of pure love flowing from him into me. Irresistibly, my arms were lifted high above my head in worship, and my doubts fled. I knew then what Isaac Watts meant by:

> *Love so amazing, so Divine,*
> *Demands my soul, my life, my all.*

The Need for Patience, Sincerity, and Submission

Those who in the past approached Pak Subuh as Bapak, with humble acceptance, received the gift of Spirit; but now that Bapak is dead, it is not an end of the matter. The opening, the *Subud* contact, is passed on undiluted by those who have already been opened in this way. The opener, in every case, merely acts as a channel for higher influences, and has nothing personal to do. Patience, sincerity and submission are keywords in *Subud*, and the quality of one's receiving depends upon heeding these qualities, because during the *latihan kejiwaan* there is nothing we can do but set aside will and desire, forget preconceptions, and be open to receive. To approach *Subud* accompanied by a mood other than one of patience, sincerity and submission, is to court disappointment and misapprehension.

Many misunderstandings have arisen through clever people "sampling" *Subud*, trying to "pick its brains". Brains may, in fact, seem alarmingly sparse to such theorisers, for at the moment of contact with higher life forces they are the least of one's concerns. If newcomers use their brains to try to understand the *latihan kejiwaan*, if they observe it and try to analyse it, they will find nothing of any value. It has no "substance". Accepted with sincerity and patience, however, the action of the *latihan* has the effect of paralysing, not thoughts and feelings themselves, but the passions, desires, prides and prejudices which normally cloak the inner feelings of man. At the opening, both the means and the potentialities are present and, provided one's habitual thoughts and desires can be relaxed or, as it were, surrendered, the receiving will follow.

Receiving the Latihan Kejiwaan

In practice it may take some time, often several months, sometimes even years, for the vibrations of the *latihan* to penetrate the hardened shell of man's innermost being, and no two people will have exactly the same experiences. Not everyone will find satisfaction, particularly if they bring their preconceptions with them into *Subud*. In some cases, the very act of desiring to receive the *latihan* – and in particular a hankering after some kind of spiritual wealth – can make actual receiving all the less likely. A powerful brain, too, can prove a hindrance; there is no doubt about that. An aim of any kind, even the noble aim of doing some good in the world, is inappropriate at this point.

Some of those hoping to follow the course of *Subud* have been disappointed with the quality of their receiving during the group *latihan*, and some have given up and left *Subud* for this reason. If, when they stand with others in the *latihan* room, they find it difficult to stop "wishing" to receive – the tension of wishing forming a barrier to the *kejiwaan* – that tension will be relieved only when the act of wishing is replaced by the realisation of itself, by the memory of wishing, by the relaxed feeling that it no longer matters whether anything happens or not. Nothing except oneself, the over-active brain, the passions, the desires, can create a barrier that precludes contact with the *kejiwaan*.

Acceptance of One's Own Contents

A few excessively moral or zealously religious people have experienced the power of the *latihan*, but have been unable to

161

accept the spiritual side of their own nature – in particular perhaps the inner nature of their own sexuality – which has seemed to fall far short of their own image of themselves. Some such people have hurriedly abandoned the *latihan kejiwaan* in some confusion, convinced that they are being assailed by an evil force – though this force is none other in fact than their own contents. Occasionally such a person will stick it out, but suppress their own contents in favour of more familiar religious or moral utterances, leaving their own true selves untouched.

Besides the mood of wishing to receive some kind of spiritual contact, the conscious effort of trying to hold thoughts at bay will also effectively preclude the action of the *latihan*. The Zen knack of no-thought must be set aside, along with the use of thoughts to stop thought. "When spring comes, the new grass grows by itself." The only things that normally prevent penetration of the contact are those perfectly correct and natural things that have been developing in us since birth: the will, the mind, the emotions. As Bapak pointed out many times, the key to receiving the *latihan* is to be found in those three simple qualities of patience, submission and sincerity – for the *latihan*, the *dharma*, is a gift which can never be taken by force.

The Nature of "Passions"

So much nowadays is heard of "passion" in every sense, that there may well be a tendency to picture it as something "apart", something that only other people have, something ungodly, perhaps, even pornographic. The word can of course mean "suffering" in the Christian sense. It can also imply romantic fiction or an enthusiasm for some special interest. But in the context of the *kejiwaan*, the passions are taken to mean the bread and breadth of everyday life – the Buddhist *samsara*. They characterise the "lower life forces" of nature as they act upon the human psyche, and they are lumped together in *Subud* vocabulary as *nafsu*. During human life on earth, the *latihan kejiwaan* is the one circumstance in which the *nafsu* has no business, and one's

162

temporary severance from these everyday passions in order to receive the movement of the *Jiwa* depends on, not suppression, but quiet submission of heart and mind, along with a relaxed attitude of "not wanting".

Spiritual Vibrations and Inner Movement

Whether the participant is aware of it at the time or not, the contact, or the subtle vibration that causes the soul of man to reawaken to life, is always present during the *latihan kejiwaan*, even when all is silent; even, indeed, when all is seemingly chaotic. Contact with Spirit will of itself split open the capsule of materiality, if one is willing to submit humbly and patiently to its power.

At the initial opening it is comparatively rare for inner movement truly to be felt immediately, and when this does happen the manifestation in oneself tends to be of a coarse nature. The lower, heavier parts of man's being have to be stirred and disturbed first, like long-stagnant water, as the soul awakes. Sometimes vibrations are felt throughout the body. Unexpected and unexplained physical movements are usually experienced, and these may be accompanied by involuntary and apparently meaningless sounds. Quite often, profanity comes to the surface, unpleasant words and gestures which some have found difficult to acknowledge as truly their own, Four hundred years before Christ, Euripides said: "'Twas but my tongue, 'twas not my soul that swore...", and now we seem to be standing his sentiment on its head. The curse that may emerge is not shallow and meaningless but deep and real, for in this case it is the soul that provides the motivations; the tongue is the innocent messenger.

Penetration of the Inner Feelings

Only at this point does it become apparent that everything one has done or thought about in the past, whether these things were good or bad in themselves, have gone to make up the contents of the lower soul, the *sukma*, now activated by Spirit and promoted to *Jiwa*. As time passes, the spiritual exercise of the *Jiwa* grows in intensity and scope, gradually becoming more subtle as the finer parts of the body and the innermost feelings are penetrated. But for the first few years, receiving takes place as a vibration exclusively via the physical body, with or without the accompaniment of speech to expel and air the feelings, and often accompanied by the smelling, hearing, or occasionally seeing of phenomena that are certainly intangible and "unscientific" – and which many, indeed, would consider hallucinatory. After a few years, receiving in the *latihan kejiwaan* is largely through the outer feelings, assisted by one's own normal voice which still declares the hidden, inner feelings. Later still, when inner and outer feelings are in balance, receiving may take place through the thinking, and may or may not be accompanied by speech. Much later still, the receiving is directly experienced through consciousness itself. Inevitably not all can live long enough on earth to see the process through to completion (if indeed that point ever occurs!), but the process will at least have been set in motion and, as it concerns the spiritual life and is not dependent upon the *nafsu* which affects our physical lives, there seems no reason why it should not continue after death.

Holding Imagination at Bay

After several years of *latihan*, when both the heart and mind have become thoroughly used to observing strange manifestations so that they come to seem almost trivial, one's attitude and actions may tend to become habitual. When the attention wanders, the coloured "brothers" of passion whose normal home is the *sukma* may try to conduct the *latihan* without the motivation of Spirit, and may even put a stop to the purifying action of the *latihan* proper. Imagination should not be allowed to play a part. It is all too easy to imagine that thoughts are being received, that one has become a fully fledged graduate while still in fact a green kindergarten pupil. In becoming careless through over-familiarity, the temptation may well occur to add "interest" by putting on a show for the "benefit" of the others present. Such vanities are plainly of no assistance to anyone. They have only nuisance value, and are bound to hinder progress in the *kejiwaan.*

The *latihan kejiwaan*, in fact, changes constantly in character, and the aspirant should remain scrupulously aware, as a sincere witness to whatever takes place within himself. Unconscious behaviour, automatism, trance, stems from some source below the kejiwaan, and below the human state. The occult world of demons has no benefit to offer, but it is not always easy to draw the line. It is during the early years in particular that the true latihan is so often accompanied by strange occult manifestations which many take to be truly spiritual. But it has been said that Spirit, and thence impersonal *Jiwa,* has no shape, colour, size or smell. Awareness of all these may come very powerfully to the inner senses during latihan, but only while the lower soul, the sukma, is still filled with the strength of the material forces.

Inner Smells : Incense and Burning Rubbish

Many *Subud* people in their early *latihan* experiences learn at first hand the true and timeless origin of incense as used in religions: the sweet "inner smell" which, without tangible source, at times seems to rise in great waves, to roll under doors, and even to spread like a flood along the street outside the place where the communal *latihan* is being held. One can well understand why religious people since ancient times have tried to recapture this strange inward smell by burning whatever will even vaguely recall it. One can experience, too, the sweet flower-like smells of death – or the death, at least, of a person with a high and noble *Jiwa* – and understand why it has become customary to gather sweet-smelling flowers for modern funeral rites.

But these smells, one suspects, have been slightly misunderstood when they are recalled – perhaps through some innate folk memory – by the priests and practitioners of so many religions both ancient and modern, as symbolic of prayer rising to heaven, selected, matched and blended in the synthetic scents of life forces above the level of humankind and above the passions. So if one has the choice, and *if* one chooses the immediate gratification and the feeling of power that familiarity with occult phenomena brings, and in thus doing rejects the higher influence of Spirit – this will comprise that one unpardonable sin: the sin against the Holy Ghost that "will not be forgiven of men". The reason why it will not be forgiven is not an arbitrary matter of judgment and punishment. But the soul that is trapped within this low material realm by choice has denied itself the possibility of that long climb through degrees of purification to a higher state, and has thereby cut off its own line of "forgiveness". Even reincarnation will be denied, as this is for unconscious, sleeping souls only. Do not forget that dreadful warning about the lake of fire and sulphur in the Revelation of St John the Divine: "This lake is the second death, and into it were flung any whose names were not to be found in the roll of the living". Like any other unpleasant spiritual experience, this is a consequence rather than a "punishment", the functioning of natural laws that have become short-circuited. It would seem a much safer choice to follow the route of submissive innocence, accompanied and guided always by the reassuring movement of the wide-awake soul, hoping eventually to "become again like a little child", even though it means parting company with these fascinating occult powers. Supernatural power was never intended for mere humans. As the psalmist wrote: "Power belongeth unto God".

Spiritual Greenness

When you close your eyes you often see colours, and such closed-eye colours tend to be of greater intensity during the *latihan*, especially in the early years. As we have seen, the *latihan kejiwaan* works through successive layers of one's inner being, and these colours are in effect a reflection of the nature of the contents currently being exposed and projected, as a film show on the screen of the receptive mind. One of the colours most often seen in this way is green, and this – the colour of the growing child within, seems to me of the greatest significance. As we have already learnt, experience may shape the form of a myth, and the vocabulary with which to express it; but the source is collective, instinctive and, in a sense, primeval. It has become fairly obvious, too, that those vivid dreams which are sometimes taken as evidence of previous incarnations, also have their origin within one aspect, one facet of the collective unconscious. I am only too well aware that "labels" such as this may mislead one into supposing that what has been labelled is already understood; but there is no doubt in my mind that this collective unconscious, brought to awareness in this case through the action of Spirit, does indeed represent the point at which all people on earth are psychically linked.

This source-book of the collective unconscious mind, representative perhaps of the *roh jasmani*, the basic human life force, is present and open within any group of people whose souls are active, as is the case during the *latihan kejiwaan* of *Subud*, And when they are being activated by or through this fundamentally human instinctual source (naturally experienced but soon abandoned in infancy), it often happens that the contents of one member become shared by the rest. Particularly when these contents reflect the concerns, the hopes and fears that have always disturbed mankind, aspects of guilt or uncertainty, quite involuntarily such features are picked up and voiced by the others present, each using his or her individual vocabulary and elaborated upon by way of the personal ideas and thought patterns associated with them.

Accumulated Faults and the Laws of Karma

Nobody has much control over his or her psychological type, and certainly none at all over inner content, which normally remains beyond the range of the mind's influence and beneath its awareness. Such contents are largely inherited, and even one's own personal faults and failings, acquired perhaps through a succession of chance incidents and mistaken attitudes during one's lifetime, are scarcely deserving of censure. Blame is a sterile charge. Plainly, nobody has ever set out to acquire encumbrances without

171

good purpose, for "every man does right in his own eyes". Whether one's personal load is heavy or light, and whether one's inner record is spotless or thoroughly blotted, depends not only on normal acquisition and inheritance. Looked at from a Buddhist viewpoint, there is the unknown factor of inheritance through countless personal reincarnations, and from any viewpoint the cause and effect of action and reaction through the boundless laws of karma. From the standpoint of certain other religions, there is the inheritance of original sin, which would seem to amount to much the same thing. And all this is quite apart from and extra to the direct inheritance of traits from one's own parents, and from more distant forebears.

Distinct from inherited faults and purely personal characteristics, are those features which have been accumulated through sexual associations with others during this life, and these can be very considerable indeed. One's inner state is liable to be fairly chaotic. But there is still no case for blame-casting, whether towards oneself or others, and to *Subud* people in particular it should come to seem quite inappropriate for any individual to harbour feelings either of guilt or resentment because of these accumulated faults. Neither would it be appropriate for anyone who aspires to *Susila Budhi Dharma* as a way of life, to deny faults which, like it or not, are his or her own.

The Process of Purification

Many human shortcomings are likely to have owed their birth to a very common and very "human" characteristic — a characteristic, needless perhaps to say, of the illusory world of *samsara*. In effect it involves the *justification* of any attitude or vanity which is not truly part of the human instinct, of the *roh jasmani* nature of an individual. Man is a lying animal, as Gurdjieff was fond of pointing out, and no man can be found who is willing to tell the whole truth about himself, in any direction, however faultless he may seem on the surface to be. Indeed, why should he be so willing? Public confessions are embarrassing and unnecessary, but of course we need to be honest with ourselves. If you "live a lie", let it be lived on the outside only. Whether consciously or subconsciously, we try to ascribe purpose to our lives and to conceal the shortcomings to which we are all heir; and this process involves continually playing a role. The role we choose to play helps either to cloak or to justify our faults. Good liars can justify almost anything, and each minor justification ties a new knot to strengthen the original trait.

To draw a clear picture of the extent of purification needful, one might imagine an interlacing network of threads woven through the fabric of the inner feelings. Gardeners will perhaps visualise a herbaceous border in which the fibrous roots of perennial plants are all thoroughly intertwined with the far-seeking fleshy roots of a choking weed such as ground-elder or couch grass. These intrusive growths might all be dislodged, given time, by means of continual shaking, tweaking, wriggling and teasing, though it would have to be done very gently to avoid breaking the brittle roots of the weed, for every fragment left in the soil will quickly grow afresh and start a new plant in its own right, making the problem worse than before. Jesus described this in slightly different terms:

When the unclean spirit is gone out of a man, he walketh through dry places, seeking rest, and finding none. Then he saith, I will return into my house from whence I came out; and when he is come, he findeth it empty, swept and garnished. Then goeth he, and taketh with himself seven other spirits more wicked than himself, and they enter in and dwell there: and the last state of that man is worse than the first.

Even if fragments of weed are not overlooked and propagated in this way, the job will take more than one season; practical organic gardeners say it takes seven years of continual work before a plot is truly free from weeds. A surer and more rapid alternative would be to lift all the plants bodily whilst they are dormant, turn them upside down and remove the network of weeds wholesale, and with comparative ease. The disruption to the bed, of course, would be total. The whole border would need reorganising and replanting in freshly prepared decontaminated soil.

173

The Spiritual Necessity of Purification

The simile can be extended from horticulture to agriculture, when in ancient times, as the parable has it, tares in a badly weed-infested crop would have to be harvested along with the wheat, and separated only in the process of threshing and winnowing. Both these extreme alternatives, of course, taken on a personal level, are analogous to death – and it will then be beyond dispute exactly who or what is "like the chaff which the wind scattereth away from the face of the earth". The alternative to death, the carefully painstaking hand-weeding, perhaps with a certain element of uprooting, represents the purification which can take place during this life on earth, on a completely involuntary basis, by the ingress of Spirit into dense layers of *sukma*, through the vibration, pulling, shaking, twisting and turning of the *latihan kejiwaan*. In this process, the aspirant at last can experience for himself or herself the difference between *Anwas* "I move", and *Anwar* "I am moved".

During the first few years of this protracted process, this "winnowing" during life, people undergoing spiritual purification can sometimes recognise in themselves – in their thoughts or behaviour – a recurrence of long-forgotten habits or characteristic features which they thought had been left behind in childhood. Indeed, there has to be a step-by-step parallel re-treading of the path followed since birth; a recapitulation of old experiences, almost in the spirit of repentance, with a corresponding correction of childish wrong turnings. This involuntary journey again through childhood can serve as a measure in charting one's current progress in the kejiwaan. It seems to happen again and again, at every change of soul-level, at every subtle death, the accumulated experiences of childhood have to be gone over repeatedly in the light of a new and yet newer understanding, a process which is not always brought to the awareness of the brain, though often spoken of in the *latihan*. The course of adulthood too has to be retraced repeatedly to the same scale of reference; one's past life "flashes before one's eyes", or sometimes lingers, unwilling to be forgotten, at each "death" of the *sukma*.

Spiritual Education

The action of the *latihan* is not always orientated towards the purification of unwanted contents. Sometimes it takes the form of a receiving of information, a taking in of matters, both spiritual and temporal, that could not be known by any ordinary means. "Snippets of information" are liable to materialise in the mouth or in the thoughts of a *Subud* member at times other than during an organised group *latihan*. They may, in fact, occur at any time when the brain is not over-occupied with day-to-day concerns. Examples of this occur very frequently, but they are often of so personal or particular a nature that there would be little point in relating them.

For the *Subud* member, previous unknown or seemingly unknowable information may become available, though not necessarily to order. One may formulate the wish to know something specific, and ask or "test" whether it is indeed so, and one may receive the answer in words, or it may be heard or seen in one way or another. It depends, I suppose, upon the individual capacity to receive the information. One soon discovers that there are all sorts of ways of seeing things that cannot normally be seen. One can quite simply and physically see and remark on something before it actually occurs, and even take evasive action as may be necessary. When driving, for instance, seeing before the event may involve being prepared to avoid an animal crossing the road, to slow down because of a prowling police car, or even to pull to the side of the road for something as potentially lethal as a runaway truck. Or you might "see" a phantasmal or wraith-like image in your mind, as for instance the inside of your fuel tank when you are about to run out of petrol, or a caricature of some person you are about to meet. These are what I would term "spiritual tricks". But you might find that you can "see" the results of some disaster which is due to befall someone you are speaking to, although circumstances forbid you to do anything about it. You are simply "seeing" the future. Numerous *Subud* members too used to "see" Bapak when, physically, he was many thousands of miles away. *Subud* members would doubtless be able to relate many other

175

examples. There is no way, apparently, that these happenings can be foreseen or brought about voluntarily, and to try to do so would be to court the occult, to be a "fortune teller"; and this would be the very antithesis of the *Subud* experience.

Repentance and Atonement

More important than this kind of "education" is the process of individual purification that is set in motion by contact with Spirit, and continues unaided. Some *Subud* members have in fact come to realise that there are distinct types of purification to be experienced during the personal *latihan kejiwaan*, depending on how deeply one's long-accumulated faults are rooted within the inner self. Firstly, there are those faults or mistakes which came about through one's own misguided or thoughtless actions in the past, and having come to light now are transferred to the outer feelings, from where they need to be purged by way of a religious feeling of positive repentance. Long-forgotten acts may return vividly to the memory, where they are seen with an objective clarity in a new light that could never previously have been suspected — particularly when dishonesty or unfairness to another person is involved, though one's actions may have seemed quite justified at the time. The memory of a wrong action such as this brings with it a sense of its enormity, followed by a deep feeling of sorrow, repentance, and often love towards the person who was wronged.

So much of normal business, professional and social life seems to involve putting another person down, taking advantage of someone, putting them in a bad light so as to enhance one's own reputation. The *latihan kejiwaan* teaches us the utter folly of this kind of act. I should stress that none of this process of recapitulation and regret is in any way voluntary, except in the sense that one must be ready to accept it. It is not really a case of "remembering" such things. Those who have experienced the depth and sincerity of such feelings brought to awareness in this involuntary way, become convinced that they occur as a way of checking the pendulum-swing of karma in our lifetime. When the

176

thinking mind is quiet and relaxed, these special memories arise at some point beyond the thinking, and become reflected, as it were, on the blank screen of the mind.

Experiencing the Practical Workings of Purgatory

In everyday life we are often made aware of "poetic justice", and find ourselves hoping that deeds good or bad may some day be appropriately rewarded by divine judgement. Now at last we can witness this process actually taking place. The expression sounds like something to be avoided, but those who "come under judgement" are the fortunate ones. For the general run of humanity, we can only surmise, retribution is likely to be delayed until after physical death – the final reaction to life's actions, as reflected in the karmic mirror held up by *Yama*, judge of the dead. Within *Subud*, this swing of the pendulum is very rapid indeed, and can even be instantaneous. If you do something even mildly "bad", or selfish, or harbour wrong thoughts in any direction, you are quickly made to regret it, one way or another. As the oft-misquoted Book of Proverbs has it, "Pride goeth before destruction, and an haughty spirit before a fall". You come under instant judgement, but no outside agency, you realise, is judging you or punishing you. Judgement comes from your own true self, and whilst *Jiwa* rules, whilst the lord of the household is at home, such judgement is immediate.

Another type of purification concerns certain non-personal faults, inexplicable in terms of memory, upbringing or experience, which seem to owe their origins to previous generations. They may even have arisen in the course of other karmic-related lives, via something very akin to the process of reincarnation. As such inherited characteristics seem quite unconnected with any personal act or omission, there is of course no way that they could be resolved through simple repentance. As far as guilt is concerned, no blame can be cast; yet they are still there as a burden for the soul. Even lesser faults which *can* be resolved through a feeling of repentance may themselves have come about not through your own wrong actions but through some inherited character defect. It is as though each seemingly unrelated incident in the past represents a separate probing root-tip of the same vast problem. It has been said that we are responsible for the welfare of our forebears as well as our own selves. Resolving the results of "sin", either through repentance or by some more subtle, impersonal working of the *kejiwaan*, to follow the gardening allegory, involves pulling up or allowing to be pulled up each individual root; and when one's individual burden is particularly heavy, the roots will be numerous and extensive, the original fault having propagated itself over and over.

Climbing Back Through Nature

All this, of course, is taking place in the context of the "lower forces", that is, within those septile divisions of the universal mandala that are beneath the horizon in the darkness of nature – the subtle world of things, of plants, and of animals – the confines of purgatory. If the lowest levels of occult influence are seen as having the nature of material objects, the next higher series of influence-levels will be seen as possessing the nature of plants, and the influence of the next set of layers will have an animal nature. One's progress through the field of the *kejiwaan* entails a steady climb through these layers of influence, starting from the bottom; and the nature, the flavour of one's personal soul-contents will reflect these differences.

The nature of animals of course is to be rootless and free to roam. It follows that all one's hypothetical roots should have been pulled up before one can progress upwards beyond the level of the plant life forces. This is not to say that any major faults originating within or beneath the plant level will have been entirely dispersed by this stage. Such faults will, however, have become rootless, loosened from the soil, and subject to being dealt with by the intelligence. Having been released from the field of the *kejiwaan*, they will to a certain measure have become free from the laws of karma and subject to one's own will, much as one has the choice of clothes and food. Their binding power, in other words, will no longer belong to the realm of the unconscious. They may linger in the mind and assert themselves through force of habit, but typically they will very soon loosen their hold and disappear.

Spiritual Crisis

Inevitably, and for any number of personal reasons, some of the faults and unwanted features which have accumulated in the inner feelings, are harder to loosen than others. Some will slip out quietly, unnoticed. Others cause the most violent disruptions, and their removal through the action of the *latihan* and the consequent raising of soul status, is sometimes accompanied by a protracted period of disturbance to the everyday routine of the person concerned. The process, and the disturbance, may continue even for years. Such a disruption within *Subud* is known as a spiritual crisis. Whilst the inner and the outer selves are in balance all goes smoothly. The two parallel scales of adjustment – on the outer, the measure of psychological change, and on the inner, the change of soul-content brought about by the *kejiwaan* – should ideally proceed at the same rate. When the difference between psychology and inner progress becomes too great, stress between the two results in crisis.

The stress of spiritual crisis may be unpleasant; but, as the contradiction of a simultaneous "yes" and "no", it is not without humour. Nor is it without wisdom. A *Subud* crisis often involves a gathering and reorientation of thoughts and impressions, and it often happens that divine truths seem to flow through the sufferer from a common source, to emerge in the form of words, or clear thoughts, or writings, which frequently explain matters hitherto regarded as mysteries. Truly meaningful books about *Susila Budhi Dharma* probably need to be written during spiritual crisis. Bapak himself remarked that his own explanatory talks to *Subud* members were a form of crisis for him. His utterances flowed through him and from his mouth, without reference to that fund of knowledge that he and each one of us have stored in the brain.

Rungs in the Ladder

More serious spiritual crises can result in bouts of physical or mental illness, occasionally severe. They may sometimes result in antisocial behaviour, seemingly quite out of character for the person concerned. They may sometimes emerge as a hypercritical attitude, or a desire to give advice – often good advice – to all and sundry. The transitional phase between adjacent life forces through or up which the aspirant must pass as a rung in the ladder, can also trigger off a protracted crisis. Often, a period ensues during which he or she is quite unable to work. Stressful periods such as this are fairly commonplace on the path of *Susila Budhi Dharma*, and the only appropriate response to them is a feeling of calm acceptance. Such things may cause difficulties for family and friends; but any rebuilding project is liable to involve inconvenience. For the majority of aspirants, for most of the time, behaviour is normal, and the minor crises of inner disruption involving the alteration and rearrangement of contents go unnoticed. But probationary members of *Subud* wishing to be opened to receive the *latihan* should be prepared to experience periods which they may well find trying. Illnesses from which they suffered in the past, perhaps during childhood, may recur, as though traces have remained to become activated by cleansing influences probing the body and vibrating the inner feelings. No two people will experience exactly the same occurrences, because the process for everyone is truly unique. It could not be otherwise.

The Uphill Path

To approach *Subud* with an open mind is actually to set foot upon the path that leads to *Susila Budhi Dharma*. Whatever names you apply to these principles, it is indeed the "narrow path" beyond religions, spoken of by prophets and patriarchs, sages and gurus. Now at last the time has come to forgo *satori*, to abandon the profitless search for *samadhi*. The reality now is that of the Zen *wu-hsin*, the unthinking spontaneity of "no-mind", the rebirth that is brought about through this *Subud* contact, the intervention of Spirit, the marvellous activity of *miao-yung*.

The guided trail is one of gradual ascent as we have seen, from the rocky chasm of material possession, through the dull worlds of plants and animals, reaching and passing through the truly human innocence of the babe in arms, to reach the saintly world of the highest. In practical terms it is full of interest: from the degradation through greed of our own and the earth's spiritual resources, through experiencing and understanding the very essence of plant and animal life, eventually to reach the human level of good stewardship, finally to reach the *rochani* level of influence to the good.

Only now can we truly understand the meaning of "satanic temptation" – in personal terms, the temptation to hold on to miraculous phenomena; the temptation, not towards any wickedness or acts of dishonesty, but to indulge in and, when the time comes, to refuse to abandon the minor miracles, the comfort, the wisdom, the fascinating activities that are the property of "black brother" – the material-level soul activated by Spirit. In non-personal terms, the temptation to continue with customs and practices harmful to world order. The temptation to refuse to modify political and industrial patterns and priorities which threaten to burden still more unequally this over-weighted zone, this base of materiality. As our inner life recovers the status of Eden, so proportionately will the earth recover. In small personal degrees, as the ball starts to roll, momentum will increase, until there need be no looking back.

Successive Layers of Soul

It would be reasonable to expect the transit of the material phase, and subsequent "soul levels", each to last seven years. But at each new stage, everything pertaining to each "brother" must be set aside as he becomes superseded, the black by the red, the red by the yellow, the yellow by the white. In each case the changeover involves death, but, as a rule, it is the "death" of the lower soul contents only while the body, the mind and the heart still live. But the changeover can still occasion a severe wrench.

181

It is only as the highest level of humanity is reached and passed that the true nature and purpose of all these seeming deaths can become apparent. *Sukma* is the seat of passion, and it is the layers of passionate being, the *nafsu*, that will have died. The four brothers who each represent a distinct aspect of the soul will effectively have shed their allegiance to the lower life forces, and no longer will they be governed by nature. They themselves will have been waiting out of sight, like a newly laundered change of clothes. Only now can their colours combine into an all-embracing brown brother whose chief characteristic is love, or compassion – a coming together of passions – a self-contained family unit able to feel and know everything that is to be felt and known, wherever its attention is directed. The repetitive cycle of death will have been completed within the living whole, and the whole soul, as *Jiwa*, need die no more.

Stressful Experiences

The greatest disruptions often seem to occur at the peak of the material level, pending transition from the *roh sjetaniah* or *raewani* of the material, to the *roh nabadi* of the plant life forces. As I have already mentioned, the wrench in this case may involve the loss of material wealth. Those who feel the least disrupted, the least abandoned at this stage, are usually those who have the coarsest contents and the most numerous faults woven into their inner feelings. These people are more likely to be made aware of what is taking place and, in practical terms, are given the strength and stamina – and the patience sometimes to rival Job – to enable them to persevere through the hiatus, by "virtue" of the sustaining strength of their interwoven faults.

Most people who travel this path will remember companions in the *kejiwaan* who have actually died during the transitional phase between material and plant levels. They have usually been people of substantial means, to whom the loss of material wealth would imply intolerable hardship. But they have also seemed particularly good people in every sense: gentle people,

182

perhaps, without any great burden of sin, excessive lust or love of materiality that might be expected to hold them to earth. This is not quite what Byron meant when he wrote: "Whom the gods love, die young". The gods in their traditional guise are usually simple manifestations of the *nafsu*, passions and desires, or archetypes of attainment within the material realm as conceived by followers of *Sahid Anwas*; so in truth this observation that "was said of yore" is stood on its head.

Material Passions Lending Strength

Perhaps I ought not anthropomorphise what may more safely be seen as a purely mechanical situation. But one's personal agents of materiality – *setans,* or spiritual entities of *roh sjetaniah* whose task it is to carry and dispose of these coarse material influences which affect the *sukma,* and which Muslims might perhaps refer to collectively as *jinn* – are able to survive the transition between life force levels. If they are coarse and heavy and powerful enough – as they probably are in the great majority of cases – these supernatural beings act as stop-gaps able to support physical life whilst the motivating strength of the *sukma* is waning or, for a brief spell, absent altogether. They are, I suppose, the driving force of *wong,* the mythical "one without soul".

Setans, then are not really undesirable, though they are sometimes lumped together as a manifestation of "Satan". As the subtle principle or workings of materiality, they account in large measure for the normal functioning of mankind, providing the physical energy, the conditioned reflexes, the automatic responses to situations, the attitudes and preconceptions which characterise any living person of a status lower at least than that of a saint. Perhaps the universal accumulation of such influences within man's being explains why the spiritual "contact" should be necessary at this time; why the process of following the *latihan kejiwaan* whilst still living on earth is usually so lengthy a business.

The Unencumbered Soul

Particularly free and childlike people, once having received the initial contact necessary for the process of purification to begin, really have no need to follow the full course on earth, as have the rest of us. With no great weight of psychological lumber to hold them down, as the material soul loses its occult solidity, there is nothing to stop the *latihan kejiwaan* continuing to work, without need of a physical form. The process is certain to be very much quicker than that experienced by the majority, who have to be twisted and shaken by the *Jiwa* every painful inch of the way. The unencumbered soul rises instantly in accordance with the appropriate level of *Jiwa,* without imbalance, through the spiritual world of the plant life forces, itself so much vaster than the visible universe; through the worlds of animal forces and human forces; through the worlds of angels and archangels. With nothing to check the expansion, there seems to be no reason why it should not fill all creation, and become one with Almighty God.

As for those remaining, we have the slow progress of the *latihan kejiwaan* here on earth, through good times and bad, through heights of spiritual purification and troughs of darkness, through heavenly joy and through depression deep enough to give rise to a wish for death. But even depression in this case is filled and paralleled with joy and bliss and thanksgiving, and death is not granted.

Gaining and Losing Wisdom

All the wealth of Solomon belongs to the material level of being, and his wisdom is inspired by that heavenly light shining through the translucent dome of the sphere of satanic forces. The ordinary aspirant to *Susila Budhi Dharma* may possess neither wealth nor wisdom; but his or her understanding too will seem to increase until the ultimate level of the material force is reached; but this is the point at which his newfound understanding falters. This is the point at which the magician on his chosen *Anwas* trail loses his powers and becomes trapped like Merlin (perhaps the Western equivalent of *Sahid Anwas* himself) in the solid rock. This is the point at which the successful *bodhisattva*, reaching the end of his physical life, finally loses consciousness to float sleeping in the sea of *nirvana*. But, following contact with Spirit and acceptance of *Susila Budhi Dharma*, the loss of understanding at this point is in fact the dawning of real understanding. The aspirant, having left the forces of materiality behind, will have risen above all that, for he knows that "he knows not". And though he finds he has entered the dark world of the *Asuras*, the unscrupulous level of the life of plants, wherein every slight and disagreement must be resolved with total destruction or total submission, it cannot influence him to the bad, for it is no longer on a higher plane than he.

Slow Passage Through the Plant Kingdom

As he enters this vastly larger inner world, the aspirant often feels it physically in his heart. Many of those undergoing spiritual purification will experience uncomfortable sensations which may last for many years, as the internal pressure and tempo of the vibration of life continually changes. Those comparatively few people who already dwell within the level of the plant forces in their normal lives, before they experience quickening of the soul, start off with a great advantage, though to them it seldom seems so. They are in no danger of "slipping away" during the transitional phase between material and plant, because no barrier exists for them. They are largely free from the lure of material wealth. In their own eyes they may seem to miss out, perhaps, by not having available to them all those strange occult experiences which may come to their fellows in the *kejiwaan* who, like the great majority of mankind, were already deep within satanic powers. It may be that they in their turn have to sink to the lower level before they can rise. But if so, they are not influenced by the material attractions that normally afflict the human race, neither are they in particular danger of dying on their return to the plant level, for their *nabadi sukma* is already developed and waiting. Nevertheless, they may well feel that they in some way miss out on the finer

from the Pandora's box of Mother Earth, only hope remains. Besides the passion of hope, the highest material-passion of faith is also present, with which to aspire to a new and truly loving human state only now appearing mistily into view.

A Time to Perceive Unity

The world is full of those who, seeing one, perceive many; few indeed are those who, seeing many, perceive but one. The time has now come for all sincere seekers to perceive that unity. One has to begin where one is. To begin by merely assuming unity in oneself, to sit hopefully within a dream of Buddha-self, is to miss the point by overlooking the many that are one. "One" may come first, with each new birth; but through the natural progress of growth and development, that one becomes many. Only much later, through grace, can that many again become one. To perceive otherwise, and at an undue time, is to incur that crippling inflation which accompanies the monkish assertion that "we are gods". Remember that this "god-like feeling...is an illusion"; a truly humble approach is more essential now than ever before. The arrogance of self-inflation blinds one to the necessary, natural disunity that, in reuniting, will form a new centre of gravity older by far than the ancient *Anwas* god of aspirant Buddhahood.

The beautiful lotus flower that floats on a foul stagnant pool will have gained its nourishment from that foulness. At death it will itself putrefy, and add to the foulness that will sustain another such flower, and after that another, and yet another, as the tranquil pool rests undisturbed, misted over with the gently stirring colours of oily putrefaction. But the bulldozer of material strength is at the gate, and the sluices are already open. Black brother operates this powerful machine, for the need to employ it can be perceived only from within the material brand of wisdom that cannot be separated from the satanic forces of the earth.

The soul of the *bodhisattva*, though subtle, has proved himself a figure of materiality. He is not, it seems, fated to achieve

188

the status even of the Green Man, and his image of oneness is no more than a dream. The "oneness wherein all things are holy" can come about only by ceasing to be a proud and holy person, by abandoning the determination to be "one" – for truly no man is an island – eventually through grace to become one in Spirit. The brotherhood within all human individuals, the passions of separate colours, black, red, yellow, and white, can now combine into the fifth and finest passion of brown brother: loving compassion; the multiple passion that bestows the ability to see and feel everything that is to be seen and felt about a person or a situation, at one and the same time.

Allowing Nature to Fall into Place

The *bodhisattva* can leave his leafy hermitage and return to civilisation with peace in his heart. The spiritual level of the plant kingdom, or the *nabadi* level of spirituality, is indeed the domain of the Green Man, and there he should be allowed to remain, bathed in occult red light. He need not be badgered into a wholly inappropriate role as a materialistic symbol for conservation. Around ancient carvings of the Green Man, truly human faces are sometimes to be glimpsed amongst his burgeoning vegetation. These are the green children – the human fruits of spiritual verdure. We are at last in a position to welcome the rebirth of a green child in each one of ourselves.

Greenness means freedom from malign influences. Spirit is not green; Spirit is pure colourless light. Fragmented soul is not green; fragmented soul is "black", "red", "yellow", or "white". Whole unified soul is not green; whole unified soul is brown – the amalgam of all souls, the basic colour of the earth over which greenery scrambles. The self that can watch and speak to and listen to these souls, to this unified soul – that self is the green child who, through our good fortune, seems destined to grow into green adulthood. When spring comes, the new grass grows by itself. When adulthood is truly green, the whole earth will flourish by itself, taking nourishment descending like dew, channelled through

189

the human, through the animal, through the plant, and into the soil, to rise again and again in clouds of wholeness.

All Things Work Together For Good

This then is the answer: to allow nature to fall into place under God-given dominion. And if our lives on earth are not long enough to see the completion of this plan, there is another dimension to it all. Death (as any religious person will be convinced) is not really the end of it. If the earth's problem is simply one of human over-population, there may be an answer there, too. Remember Bapak's explanation to the Buddhist enquirer: "Reincarnation is what happens to people who do not follow the *latihan kejiwaan*". He has also said: "Heaven is work". Do not think that one who has exceeded the earth's bounds and the bounds of the *rochani* has become inactive or irrelevant to the earth and its needs. The idle ghost of *nirvana* can be laid once and for all. Such a person will have acquired awareness of all matters, and everything can fill his consciousness. Spiritual influence is part of the process of creation, and it has been said that this process, delegated, provides employment for the few when their apprenticeship in the *kejiwaan* is complete.

But our aim is not some speculative afterlife. Our sights are not set upon death. If enough people with worldly influence take to the *latihan kejiwaan* theirs will be influence to the good, and in the words of St Paul: "We know that all things work together for good to them that love God, to them who are called according to his purpose". There is no need for us to lose our own strength of purpose, or to sacrifice the power of our minds; these can be recruited. A shift of viewpoint is needed, through the power of reason rather than blind religious acceptance. The theory is of no real value. The name doesn't matter; the language doesn't matter; the hierarchy doesn't matter. Practical, personal experience is all that counts. As an alternative, we can continue to pit our wits one against the other as we watch the world die. If man lives by nature, nature has her own solutions to bad stewardship, and they are not pleasant to consider. The Apocalyptic horsemen of war, famine, pestilence and death are mounted and ready.

The Last Chance?

Propaganda has never been appropriate to *Susila Budhi Dharma*. It is not something that can be handed out like a bowl of rice or a condom, or something that can be seized upon by the underprivileged, the desperately poor, or the starving. It is of no use either to the racist lout, or the self-obsessed hedonist, or the narrow-minded revolutionary. The overly strong-minded and self-confident will not take kindly to it. It is for the ordinary, comfortably-off, mild mannered people who care about the world and its problems to take up this final challenge. No change of lifestyle is called for. No esoteric knowledge is required. The way may be rough for the individual, but it is the *only* way. Our own past actions have made us all an inheritance which now has to be paid for. But however harsh any penalty might seem, it is the soul above all that knows fulfilment. "Though pangs and sorrows may still come through past misdeeds, all suffering is made bearable through the joy of Spirit". If we fail in this, we may not get another chance.

The Spiritual Path

Inspired by the Javan song-poem *Susila Budhi Dharma*
of Muhammad Subuh Sumohadiwidjojo

In ancient times did Adam's wilful child
Pursue his dharma deep in forests wild.
Lone monks on mountain tops would meditate;
On haunted seashore; lonely river ait;
      Nourished perchance by falling autumn leaves.
But from such wilderness grew farm and industry
And bustling harbour, grimy factory,
Once empty beaches echoing childhood glee
      So man it seems his destiny achieves.

So through their ancient fables men sought grace,
Or pinned their hopes on such and such a place,
Through pilgrimage to building, shrine, or stone
Sought by satanic forces to atone:
      A holy place is but a thing of clay.
Would dreamers, scanning skies for godly signs,
Whilst scholars scrutinise some holy lines
By gutt'ring candle, fathom God's designs,
      God's mysteries revealed by light of day?

Where was that forest wild but in the mind?
Within our heart, that mountain top we find.
That desolate shore to which the fakir came
Witnessed the anguish of his tortured frame.
      Perceptions, understandings, change at length.
That mighty river where the hermit stayed
Along whose course the chuckling ripples played
Served but to mock his passions unallayed.
      Those bodily desires live on in strength.

That forest of the mind still tangled grows.
That ocean of sensation overflows.
That mountain of the heart seems higher yet.
That river flows as ever, still in spate.
      Ascetic deeds of ancient times are past.
The truth is here, along this busy street.
Let symbols go; their purpose is complete.
All sons and daughters, races, creeds, can meet.
      Divine reality is yours at last.

GLOSSARY

About Words

As the Hindu Teaching has it:

Our minds are in confusion over matters of the soul because of the endless contradictions of our teachers – because of the imperfection of words.

Sometimes an unfamilar word or phrase can make more sense than a familiar one, simply because we are trying to describe some new or unfamiliar concept. If we use a familiar description, the implication is that we already understand whatever is being described. In *Greening of the Soul* I have borrowed words from various sources because English words cannot adequately describe the issues raised. Probably, neither can words borrowed from the Sanskrit, from Sufi tradition, from Javan mythology, from Arabic, from Moslem or Hindu or Buddhist or Christian tradition, or any other source, do any better. Religious emotion can serve no purpose; passions and desires will prove counter-productive. Modern psychological terms too are out of place: spiritual experience is not be arrived at through exploring the layers of mind. The point is, spiritual matters have no solid, material basis which can be analysed or made logical, and the path of *Susila Budhi Dharma* is indeed a spiritual one, though it applies to us here and now, living in our own real, solidly material bodies.

It may well be that my choice of descriptive words in this book will seem offensive or aggravating to some readers, for various reasons. My own experience in *Subud* has shown me that this is likely. Intellectual people in particular do tend to suppose that because a word has a certain origin, it can have no meaning beyond its own cultural ambience, its own world view, its own religious or philosophical background. The solution is simple: If a word offends you, pluck it out, or, at least, change it for one that you prefer. Words are just words.

Anwar	Submissive or obedient, in the spirit of the mythical character *Sahid Anwar.*
Anwas	Wilful or assertive, in the spirit of the mythical character *Sahid Anwas.*
Aras Allah	The Seat of God: that part or principle of a person that becomes able to receive higher influences.
asura	In Buddhist mythology, a fierce demonic being here representative of the plant life forces.
Bapak	Father; in Indonesia a respectful reference to an elder. Specifically referring to Muhammad Subuh Sumohadiwidjojo.
black brother (or sister)	That aspect of the human soul that is inspired by the life forces of materiality.
bodhisattva	One who aspires to be a Buddha.
brown brother (or sister)	That aspect of the human soul that represents a condition of wholeness.
budhi	The condition of being spiritually alive.
crisis	Here taken to mean a psychological disturbance brought about by spiritual changes.
dharma	One's true God-given nature.
dhyana	True human instinct, without modification by heart and mind.
hakekah	Islamic wisdom that lends spiritual reality to the sharia.
hatha yoga	A type of yoga that concentrates mainly on bodily control.
jasmani, jasmaniah	The spiritual life force particularly appropriate for human beings.
Jiwa	The higher human soul, having been inspired by Spirit.
karma	The spiritual law of cause and effect.

kejiwaan	"Of the Jiwa": the spiritual field in general.
khewani, khewaniah	The spiritual life force particularly appropriate for animals.
koan	In Zen, a form of riddle involving spontaneity.
kundalini	In yoga, said to be a force rising from within.
latihan kejiwaan	Spiritual exercise experienced by people who have been opened in *Subud*.
mandala	A circular (or sometimes square) symbol of the universal principle, and equally of the self in search of oneness.
miao-yung	Spontaneous marvellous activity recalled by Taoists.
nabadi, nabadiah	The spiritual life force particularly appropriate for plants.
nafsu	Desires and impulses; every influence that originates below the truly human level.
nirvana	In Buddhism, the cessation of passions.
Pak	Bapak; in Indonesia used as a term of address for an elder.
purgatory	The ongoing process of spiritual purification, recognised particularly by the Catholic Church.
Qadr	Contact with the life forces of spirituality, as described by the Prophet Mohammed.
rabbani, rabbaniah	The highest spiritual life force of the seven.
raewani, raewaniah	The spiritual life force pertaining to the world of materiality.
rahmani, rahmaniah	The second highest spiritual life force of the seven.
red brother (or sister)	That aspect of the human soul that is inspired by the life force of plants.
rochani, rochaniah	The spiritual life force directly above that appropriate for humans.
roh, roch	A spiritual life force.

Sahid Anwar, Sahid Anwas	Two brothers of Adam in Javan mythology.
samadhi	In Buddhism, a trance-like state of oneness.
samsara	In Buddhism, the ordinary world of sensations.
satori	The Buddhist principle of enlightenment.
septile division	In astrology, the seventh part of a circle, here relating to one partition of the universal mandala.
setan, shetan	A principle of material energy affecting the human condition.
sharia, shariah	Islamic law and religious devotion in practice.
sjetani, sjetaniah	The "satanic force", spiritual life force of materiality.
Subud	A shortened form of *Susila Budhi Dharma*, an organisation dedicated to passing on contact with higher spiritual life forces.
sukma	The lower human soul, or "astral body", as distinct from the higher spiritual soul or Jiwa.
susila	Living according to one's dharma.
Tao	In Chinese philosophy, the spiritual principle, or the way back to the source.
white brother (or sister)	That aspect of the human soul that is inspired by human life forces.
wong	A person or condition of life bereft of spiritual content.
wu-hsin	In Zen, "no-mind", a condition of spontaneity.
Yama	In Buddhist mythology, judge of the dead.
yellow brother (or sister)	That aspect of the human soul that is inspired by the life forces of animals.

INDEX

mythological images 170

nature, life forces of 20, 26, 27, 35,
36, 38, 87, 113, 114-117
nirvana 19, 96, 128

occult 166
opening the soul 104, 105, 149, 153,
163

Pan 30
passions, soul 130-132
Paul, Saint 38, 190
persona 22
plant life force 20, 26, 27, 87, 113,
114-117
religion 28, 29, 49
poems:
African Capricorn 9
Behold the rhino 36-37
Bodhisattva 105
Brothers and sisters 77-78
Dharma 155
Garden of God 95
Green Man 32
Human soul 40-41
Ikebana 13
Jacob's ladder 122-125
Lights of rebirth 107-110
Nature of Zen 51
Passions 91
Reincarnation 92
Shadow 54
Song of the Tao 44
Spiritual path 192
Still small voice 149-150
Victim soul 24-25
Yogi 71-72
Zodiac 57-59
purgatory 177
purification 172-174, 177, 178

Qadr 88, 103, 151

racial attitudes 77-80

rebirth 106, 121
cyclical 56, 63
reincarnation 92-101, 111
religious attitudes 18-20, 25, 25, 26
repentance 178
Revelation of John 50, 76, 168
revenge, nature of 20
ritual 135

samsara 126, 129
Satan 22, 35
satanic power 15, 118, 126
satori 56, 63, 82, 102
self analysis 55
setans 183
sexual content 53, 54, 55
shadow, psychic 22, 54
Shakyamuni 106
Shantideva 104, 105
Shorea robusta 21
smells, inner 165, 166
soul, artificial 64, 73, 74
awakening 103, 104
contents 53
instinct 11
nature of 17
opening 104, 105, 149, 153, 163
spiritual decline 30, 86-89
spontaneity 83, 84
Subud 11, 16, 39, 84, 91, 106, 148,
151, 157, 158, 159-191
Subuh, Muhammad 11, 38, 49, 73, 81,
88, 106, 134, 146, 148, 159, 160
sukma 98, 146
susila budhi dharma 9, 11, 17, 19, 50,
90, 104, 159-191

Tao 83
thoughts and emotions 75, 76, 99, 155
tongues, speaking in 154

unconscious, personal or collective
64, 158, 171
Upanishads 47, 50, 93, 97, 126,
135-145

And I say unto you, Ask, and it shall be given you; seek, and ye shall find; knock, and it shall be opened unto you.

Gospel according to St Luke, Chapter 11

www.dreamstairway.co.uk

Made in the USA
Lexington, KY
09 June 2010